Yacht Club to Diamond Mine

My Journey to Working at One of Walt Disney World's Most Popular Attractions

Conor Brown

Theme Park Press
The Happiest Books on Earth
www.ThemeParkPress.com

Theme Park Press publishes its books in a variety of print and electronic formats. Some content that appears in one format may not appear in another.

Editor: Bob McLain
Layout: Artisanal Text

ISBN 978-1-68390-207-2
Printed in the United States of America

Theme Park Press | www.ThemeParkPress.com
Address queries to bob@themeparkpress.com

CONTENTS

Yacht Club to Diamond Mine

Introduction

Who exactly is this book for?

It's for you! That's why you picked it up of course.

I tried to write this book for anyone and everyone. Now I know I can't try to appeal to everyone all of the time. But I think there are aspects of this book that can appeal to a lot of different people.

If you're interested in learning about the Disney College Program and want to see if it's something you want to do then this book is for you.

If you're about to start your Disney College Program and you want some insight into what it's like then this book is for you.

If you just want to see what it's like working at the Vacation Kingdom of the World then this is the book for you.

If you're a crazy Disney fan, like me, and you just crave any Disney World content you can get your hands on then this book is for you.

If you are interested in learning more about me... wait, really? You actually want to know more about me? Well I am flattered and a little perplexed but regardless, this book is for you!

I spent almost a full year working at the Walt Disney World Resort just outside Orlando, Florida. It was a dream of mine for as long as I can remember. I learned more about myself in that year than probably any other year before or since. When I set out to write this book I thought I had a unique story to tell. One that hadn't ever really been told before. For one it was my own story but I also took a path that not many people actually take while working at the resort. I thought it would be a unique perspective that people would like to see.

As I started to write the book I realized that while my story was unique and interesting I actually also had experiences and tips that I thought people could benefit from learning. Lessons and techniques I learned and came to realize that might actually help people in their daily lives. It might seem weird because all I really did was work at a theme park. But for whatever reason the things I experienced helped me in ways I could never imagine.

As you read this book I hope you're entertained. I hope you find the story enjoyable and insightful. But I also hope you learn something. Sure, I hope you learn about the Disney company and how it operates but, I hope you learn something that can help you in your own daily life, too.

So who is this book really for then? I guess it's for the curious. If you want to learn and have a curiosity to do so, then this is the book for you.

CHAPTER ONE

Destined to Work Here

"Paging Mr. Morrow. Mr. Tom Morrow."

I remember exactly where I was when I found out that I could work at Walt Disney World. I was riding on the Tomorrowland Transit Authority PeopleMover at the Magic Kingdom. My head rested on my arms as I watched Tomorrowland go by from the blue and silver omnimover.

"You know I use to work on this ride.", said my Mom who was seated next to me.

My ears perked right up. "You what?" I responded surprisingly. "I use to work here, I did something called the Disney College Program during one summer in College. I worked on this ride and the Astro Orbiter right above us", she said.

Up until that point I guess I just had never realized that actual people worked at Walt Disney World. To me the cast members were just a bunch of incredibly lucky people who got to work at my favorite place in the world. As a middle schooler I really never thought about work other than imagining working in some occupation like as a vet, firefighter or something little kids often dreamed about.

I started to press my Mom on what this magical Disney College Program was. She explained how she moved down to Orlando for a summer and was able to work in the parks, take a class and get paid while earning credit for College. It sounded too good to be true and as I started to think about it I noticed how some cast member's name tags said Colleges or Universities instead of what towns they were from. It must still exist!

As soon as my trip was over I did a quick search for the Disney College Program during my allotted computer time of the day. Yeah it was all above my head but, the idea, the notion that I could one day work at Disney World was implanted in me. I was determined to make that dream a reality even if it was six years before I could even go to college let alone apply for the program.

Imagine that. Before I knew what I wanted to do, before I knew what I wanted to study, before I even knew where I wanted to go to College I knew I wanted to be a part of the Disney College Program. In High School I remember filling things out saying I was an interested college student who wanted to know more about the program just so I could gain access to videos that discussed it more in depth. I was obsessed. Time was my biggest enemy in my quest. It wasn't ever a question of how I was going to work there it was just a question of when.

This obsession was pretty much par for the course though in my love of all things Disney and especially Disney World. My first trip was when I was three and was followed quickly by a second trip a year later. My Mom had been to Disney World before, obviously when she was on the college program but here first time was as a child when she stayed in the Contemporary Resort during the first few years of Walt Disney World being open. My Dad had never been before but quickly got hooked. Our trips occurred every other year and it's hard to pinpoint when exactly my obsession began to form but 8th grade is probably a safe bet. It was then that my parents decided to buy into the Disney Vacation Club. They saw it as a great way to secure Disney vacations for the family, which now also included my sister, for years to come. Our trips quickly became an annual occurrence.

For most the allure of Disney World wears off as you grow but it definitely had the opposite effect on me. My love of the place only grew, and continues to grow, as I get older. In High School I began to help plan our trips. Picking which resort it would be cool to stay at, what new restaurants we should try out and what park to go to on which days. The times between my trips I filled consuming as much Disney World content as possible. Reading articles, scouring through message boards and exploring YouTube videos for anything and everything I could find. I was determined to learn as much about the place as I possibly could.

The more I found out about the details and the history of the company the greater my interest grew. Disney was a part of America and Disney World has become an almost rite of passage for many families. With each trip I gained a greater appreciation for the place and a great appreciation for the cast members that worked there. My desire to work at Disney World changed from a place of me wanting to working their because I thought I would have a great time to wanting to work there as a way for me to give back. It might sound weird to want to work at Disney World to give back but, my mindset was that if so many cast members worked hard to make my trips so great then I should try to do the same.

My mission was simple. I was going to work at Disney World because I loved it and I wanted to give others the great experiences I had encountered. Nothing was going to stop me on that quest. I was destined to work there after all.

My destiny lead me to get to work at the most magical place on earth. Little did I know that same destiny would send me on a roller coaster (both figuratively and literally in the form of Seven Dwarfs Mine Train!) of an experience. An experience complete with two roles, two apartments, 11 different roommates and countless memories. The best of those memories I'll try to explain here while I recount my time spent and lessons learned working at Walt Disney World.

Ready for an adventure? Let's get started.

CHAPTER TWO

The Process

The time had finally come. A moment I had been waiting for every since I was in middle school. It was my time to apply for the Disney College Program. I had waited until I was a senior in college partly because I had also decided to study abroad and I couldn't afford to be away from campus for another semester if I wanted to graduate on time. While you can take classes on the program and earn college credit while doing it, it won't come close to the amount you'd earn during a normal semester at your school's campus.

Luckily one can apply for the Disney College Program during their final semester of college and participate in it after they graduate. You need only to be in school while you apply. So it was settled, come the second semester of my senior year I'd apply.

It was incredibly risky. At the time it didn't ever cross my mind but now I see how things could've easily gone horribly wrong. I basically gave myself one shot at accomplishing my dreams. I only applied once and only applied at the very last opportunity I would have. The program is competitive to get into and I could have easily been denied and with it my chances at working at Disney World. Some often apply two, three or even four times before they are accepted.

I was nervous about being accepted but I was also confident. That's why when the application window opened

I applied as quickly as I could get to my computer. The process of applying is broken into three different components. The first is filling out the application itself. It's part job application part college application. You fill out basic information, education information and answer certain questions about the program itself. Those last questions revolve around what program you want to apply for (Disney World, Disneyland or both) and what roles you would be willing to work in. There's close to twenty roles you can select from. For each role you select your level of interest and state whether you'd be willing to work in the role at all.

Once you submit the application most immediately move onto the next phase in the process, the web based interview. I should note that getting to this stage isn't always guaranteed but it's definitely the easiest of the stages to get to. If you pass you'll receive an email to complete the web based interview. This can be done at any time but must be done in one-sitting. This is basically like a robust personality test, you're asked how do you handle stress, do you work well with others, etc. The key here is to answer truthfully and consistently as many questions are very similar but just asked a little differently. This is Disney's way of testing to see if you're really up for the task.

Through the application process there are only two enemies you have. Time and yourself. Disney is not looking to find as many people as possible. They need the workers and they want to find as many people as possible. But they also know that finding the right talent is more important than finding the largest amount of talent. For their brand to succeed it starts with the talent they hire. That's why your biggest enemy is time and yourself.

Time you have no control over. It will eat at you and the longer the process takes the more down you can get on yourself. Nothing good will ever come worrying about time and letting the wait eat at you. Keep your head up and have a good attitude about it. The more you worry the harder it will be to continue in the process. Especially if you get to the phone based interview.

This is the toughest nut to crack. Many get to it but few make it past. This is where Disney takes your responses and puts a voice and a personality to the application. You'll speak with an interviewer and the key here is to give clear and concise answers while showing a passion and a personality that Disney not only wants to see but needs to see. Here's where you can really be your own worst enemy. The best thing to do in the interview is take a deep breath and focus on smiling (You really should smile as you answer the questions. It might sound crazy but people can hear you smiling as you answer the questions. It shows you are excited for the opportunity too.) and showing your best side. Easier said than done but as long as you believe in yourself you can do it.

Once you get through the phone interview the time aspect starts to kick in again and the waiting game continues. If you're about to apply to the program I have a couple of tips to make this process easier for you. One tip is to just try and occupy your time with things other than Disney and the process. Being in school helps this effort but constantly refreshing your email or online application dashboard won't help anything.

Around this time you'll probably start to join Facebook groups filled with other eager applicants who are also anxiously awaiting their fate. A word to the wise, participate in these groups with caution. Every new post of someone being accepted can only add to the burden of waiting. It can feel like everyone is getting accepted but you. When you see a post of someone getting accepted you of course then proceed to click on the profile of the individual. After looking over their profile you will inevitably say to yourself, "how did this person get accepted and I haven't yet!!". Ok....maybe that's something I did but, I'm sure others have as well. It's easy to compare ourselves to others but, being consumed wondering why certain people got in and you haven't won't help you in the long or short run.

The Facebook groups are great for finding roommates once accepted or asking questions to get other people's opinions. Where it doesn't help is when it becomes a place for someone to brag that they were accepted and for others to lament about how they weren't. The sob stories of the people who just got denied are just bad energy you don't need to experience. It sucks that not everyone makes it but, that's the nature of the beast. You can get sucked into the sob stories and lose confidence in yourself with the success stories. Join these groups but also be wary of them

Take my word on these accounts because this is coming from a guy who's been down this path. I got through every stage as quickly as I could only to have to wait until the very final day of the application window to discover my fate.

Obviously it turned out good or I wouldn't be writing this book! I was accepted and got my second choice for the role I wanted. My first choice was Concierge, I thought i'd love this as I'd just be helping plan guests stays. I'd answer their questions, book dining reservations for them, assist with their ticket needs and give them my insider knowledge of tips as someone who had been visiting Disney World for years. Alas, that was not meant to be. But the role I was accepted for wouldn't be too far away. I'd be working as a Front Desk cast member at one of the onsite Disney hotels.

I'd check-in guests and help them with difficulties they might run into during their stay. I wouldn't find out my actual hotel location until I got down there but I was more than happy with the role.

My fate was sealed. I'd be graduating in May and moving to Orlando in August. It was incredible to think that the moment I had been waiting for, for years and years was finally in arms reach.

CHAPTER THREE

Getting There

I had a whole summer ahead of me before I would make my trek down to Orlando but, I had plenty to do. There were things to buy, hotels to book and logistics to plan out. Luckily coming from the college environment I was able to bring most of the items I used in my dorm rooms down with me which would fit in perfectly to my new apartment.

Apartments on the program are pretty standard. Their double occupancy rooms meaning two people share one bedroom. There even is the option to have three to a bedroom. I never saw one of these in person but having experienced what the normal double is like, I can only imagine how cramped a triple must feel. Furniture is included as well as the kitchen being stocked with pots, pans, cutlery and utensils. Which was great since I would really only be responsible for bringing clothes, toiletries a T.V. and maybe a few other things.

I had asked my Mom if she would make the trip with me from our home in Maryland all the way down to Central Florida and luckily she said yes. After reading many horror stories about the buses available to college program students I opted to bring down my car. The trip was long but having my car while on my program more than made up for it. Plus having my Mom on the trip down made it a whole lot easier.

The drive itself was surreal for me. Here's something I've wanted to do my whole life, or at least as long as I can remember. I had finally been given the chance to do it and I was almost there. Yet, in the back of my head I couldn't help but think of things that might go wrong. What if I didn't like my role, or my location was awful, what if my roommates sucked and made apartment life miserable and on top of all that what if I didn't make any new friends.

Now it may seem crazy to think about not making new friends in a program that welcomes thousands of new cast members my age every single season but it was something that began to consume me. What you have to realize is I had just graduated from college a few months before. I had to say goodbye to some of my best friends that I had spent the last four years with. They lived all over the country and saying goodbye to them and to the place I had called a second home for four years was difficult. Then just a short time later it was like I was starting all over again. It can be a daunting task in an emotionally filled time.

A word to the wise who want to participate in the college program. You might feel like you can't do this and you might feel like you want to give up. When those feelings come over you stop, take a deep breath and keep going. We all get homesick or emotional and when it inevitably happens just acknowledge it and to quote a cold ice Queen, "let it go". My emotions almost got the best of me but I knew I'd be letting myself down if I didn't go through with this thing that I'd been wanting to do my whole life. You can't plan for everything in life and you're better off going with the flow then trying to control the uncontrollable.

My emotions at ease I was off to Orlando.

CHAPTER FOUR

The Arrival

I was thinking about naming this Chapter D-Day as so much happens on your first day on the program. You wake up super early, make the trek over to the Vista Way apartment complex and then you wait in line with a bunch of other eager college programmers checking-in. It's here where you will find out what location you'll be working at, you'll get your schedule for the first week and you'll discover what apartment complex you'll be living in. A little later on when you first make your way to the apartment you'll find out who your roommates are.

For some they are able to find roommates before they arrive in Orlando. Either because their friend is doing the program at the same time or they find others online. Typically through the Facebook groups.

It use to be that if you wanted to live together with people you had to get in line with them at the same time at check-in. Then you would tell the cast members at check-in what you're housing preferences are and how you'd like to live with these individuals. If there was availability in the place you wanted you would get it. If not you would need to compromise on either the occupancy or the apartment complex.

Luckily in the last few years the college program has been able to streamline this and make it apart of the pre-arrival process. The Disney Onsite Resident

Management System (DORMS) is what you use before you arrive to fill out housing information and indicate apartment and roommate preferences. Because of this you don't need to get in line with your roommates in order to room with them. There is no guarantee that your preferences will be met, but Disney will do its best.

I went random when it came to roommates. In preparing for the program I read through countless blogs and what I came across was a pretty even split of good versus bad roommate situations. Sometimes everyone got along great and other times people didn't mesh well. I realized that there was no correlation between this and if they went with random roommates or had decided to live with them before arriving.

I've always been cautious about selecting people to live with when all you know is there social media profiles. A profile does not make the person and there's plenty that never makes a profile for people. That can be good or bad. You could judge them by their profile and think you wouldn't get along and they actually turn out great or you could see their profile and think they'd be a good match and then you met them to discover they aren't. Of course there's always the option when they look good and are good but you get what I'm saying. There's no definitive way of knowing.

With that, and the stories I had read, I decided to press my luck! I would be put in with random roommates. Which when you think about it really is a crazy concept. The day before check-in I went to bed not knowing who I'd be sharing a room with the next night and for the next five months. Crazy, right?! But it is a good kind of crazy. It can help push you out of your comfort zone which I think is always a good thing.

Now let's talk apartment complexes.

Currently there are four locations available to college programmers: Vista Way, Chatham Square,

Patterson Court, and the Commons. Each has their pros and cons and you should take them all into consideration. What I would focus on is how many roommates you want to live with and factor in if you will be bringing a car (if you have the opportunity to bring a car you 100% should). Apartments are broken out by bedroom and occupancy. Most bedrooms are double occupancy but there are triple options. The triple rooms, from what I've been lead to believe, have one bunk bed and an additional twin where as the doubles just have two twins.

Occupancy and which complex you live in determines your rent. Staying at an older complex like Vista Way will be cheaper than staying at a newer one like the Commons. Staying in a three bedroom will be cheaper than staying in a one bedroom. My advice here, look at prices and see what you are comfortable with but don't let that be your main factor when choosing the complex and apartment size. If you are going on the Disney College Program with the sole intent of making money, you're going to be let down. You'll make money but you won't be getting rich. The perfect price point is the one that makes you the most comfortable.

I would recommend going for a two bedroom or three bedroom option. I stayed in two different three bedroom units with five other roommates. That many people in there is a lot. A four bedroom obviously has eight people in it and while there's an additional room everything else can be quite tight. There may be one more bedroom but there's only one kitchen and one common area to share amongst eight people. That can get crazy. A one bedroom sounds great but if you end up not liking your one roommate it can feel debilitating to go home. A few more people will help you branch out.

Now I'm sure it can get overwhelming with all this info but it's important to do your research. Think about what you're going to be doing. You're moving to Orlando, it might be your first time living somewhere new, you're going to be living with total strangers for the next five months (or longer) and you're going to be living in one apartment for that amount of time too. You want to prepare so that you can have the best opportunity for success.

For me, planning was also a way to build anticipation. With each new step I took I would only get more and more excited. Curious about where I was going to live, who I was going to live with and where I was going to work. It's all very exciting.

With everything in order the day finally came for me to check-in. It was August 17, 2015. I was one of the first groups to check-in through the new process of pre-selecting what complex you'd like to live in. Up until then it was almost like a first come first serve basis. People would wait outside check-in starting at 5 or 6 a.m. waiting for the gates to open. They would do this to try and guarantee that they got their first preference of housing. Luckily for me I wouldn't have to wake up so early. The new pre-arrival process really helped in this regard. The new process gives you an arrival time frame to show up to try and alleviate congestion. Mine was from 11:45 a.m.-12:45 p.m. I could show up at anytime during then to hop in line.

It was a nice relaxed morning. My mom and I were staying at Disney's Old Key West Resort and we had breakfast at the restaurant there named Olivia's. We got to talking to our server and I told him how I was about to go check-in for the college program. He was excited for me and gave me some tips. Then at the end of the meal he brought us the check and said, "since you're basically becoming a cast member today I went ahead and gave you the cast member discount for the meal". Talk about some Disney magic!

After breakfast I really couldn't wait any longer so we drove over to Vista Way which is where the check-in process takes place. My time had come so I walked through the gates and got in line. My mom went to the parent waiting area which was really just some picnic tables outside one of the buildings. The check-in process can take a little while. While Disney has several arrival dates split up over different weeks for each new session, many hundreds of people can still be checking in on any given arrival day.

As you wait in line you'll inevitably start talking to people around you. The typical small talk, Where you from? What school do you go to?, will ensue but then the Disney talk will quickly take precedent. What's your role? Where do you want to work? What apartment complex do you want to be in? It was cool to be surrounded with so many people from all walks of life.

I also had a lot of time to think in line. Thinking about how this program was going to play out and where I was going to work. But I also had other thoughts. It's hard to describe but, I had been waiting for this moment my entire life. It was surreal to think that it was actually here, that I was checking-in for my program and my career was going to begin. In a time span of three months I had graduated college, said goodbye to my friends at school then said goodbye to my friends back home, packed my car up and moved to Orlando. The feeling was incredible. I had accomplished my goal of getting there. Sure I was nervous about things and about how it was all going to work out but I made it, I was here. That's all I had ever wanted.

Before I knew it I was at the front of the line. Check-in consists of a lot of stuff they just have to get out of the way. You'll get your parking tags for your car, you'll get your photo taken and your housing I.D., you'll have to sign some paperwork among other things. But the real exciting part of check-in is finding out what complex you'll be living in and where you will be working.

The time had finally come to find out where I was going to be working!

To be honest I really didn't have a preference of what resort I wanted to work at. Sure I thought there were a lot of cool ones but there wasn't one that stuck out that I felt I needed to work out. There were ones I did not want to work out though...

The All-Star Resorts are in the Value Category of Disney Resort Hotels. They are more affordable but their amenities aren't as nice as the Moderate or Deluxe levels. Now I didn't really care about what level I would be working at I had just heard horror stories about the All-Stars. They are MASSIVE resorts. I had stayed at them before and I would often notice how long the lines were at check-in. It just seemed like chaos to me. Since I had originally had this thought I have talked to co-workers who had worked at the All-Stars before and some of them loved it. It's definitely still a cool place to work, just at that time I didn't want to have anything to do with them.

I gave my information to the cast member and she said, "Ok, ready to find out where you'll be working?" I responded, "I've been waiting my whole life for this sister." (Alright, I didn't actually say that but it would've been pretty cool if I did.) "You'll be working at...." my inner monologue at this time was: "Please not the All-Stars, please not the All-Stars, please not the All-Stars". "You'll be working at the Yacht & Beach Club Resorts!" I can get behind that. I had stayed at the Beach Club before and I've always loved the Epcot Resort area where it's located so I was more than ok with that. Work location discovery complete.

Now just to find out where I'd be getting my beauty sleep for the next few months.

Going in I also didn't really have a preference of where to live. I had my car so transportation would be easy for me. I knew of the reputations each complex had but that didn't really bother me. I put my preferences as any two or three bedroom in any complex. I got placed in a three bedroom in Vista Way. I can deal with that! There's a Chick-Fil-A right next door for crying out loud!

Since I was already in Vista Way I made my way over to the apartment to see who was there. Three roommates had already shown up by the time I had gotten there. I took the empty bed in the room occupied by one of them. We had two others we were still waiting on. You never really know who's going to walk through the door until they do. Luckily the two remaining guys were two of the best guys I've ever met. The roommate situation had its ups and downs but I think for the most part it wasn't too bad. My immediate roommate who I shared the room with was great.

The rest of the day was occupied with moving in, making trips to Wal-Mart and just trying to settle in. It was a whirlwind of a day and by the end of it I was exhausted. My roommates decided to go out to dinner together but since it was one of my mom's last nights there I decided to hang out with her.

Here I was. Moved into a new apartment with new roommates knowing where my new job location would be. The adventure had begun.

CHAPTER FIVE

Training

You're first few days on the program aren't spent at your location. That comes later. First you need some basic Disney training. Training times vary from role to role and location to location. I was fascinated by the training process. Just the sheer logistics of training alone is incredible. As someone who has been going to Disney World forever, anytime I can learn something new about the resort I always get excited. With training I got my first taste of what life backstage would be like.

The first step is going to Casting. Casting is the HR and hiring building basically. But since we put on a show at Disney World, complete with cast members, backstage areas, etc. it's called Casting. You find out when your time to go to Casting is when you arrive at check-in. Groups go at different times to alleviate the masses at the building but typically you'll go within the first few days of your arrival.

Casting is an awesome building. It's right across from Disney Springs and its architecture is very cool. When I stepped inside that building for the first time I was overcome with emotions. Good emotions! Lots of happiness. I was happy that I was finally here.

Your time at Casting is filled with doing paperwork, getting your fingerprints taken and having a brief overview of the company. Pretty standard stuff. But I think it's a cool introduction to everything.

The real training begins with Traditions which takes place at Disney University located behind the Magic Kingdom. This is where most of the pre-location training takes place. If you haven't heard of Traditions before it's the orientation that every Disney cast member goes through. It covers the history of the company, what it stands for and what defines the organization today. If you were on the fence about whether you liked this company or not, you definitely won't be once you go through Traditions. As a die-hard Disney fan it was an awesome experience.

Its main focus is on the Four Keys. The Four Keys are Safety, Courtesy, Show and Efficiency in that order. These are what each cast member needs to focus on when performing their job. They want to make sure what they are doing is safe. Then each guest must be treated with courtesy. Remember when I said we were all putting on a show? That's where the show key comes in. To remember what Disney World stands for and play our part in the show. Then we want to do things in an efficient manner. This is both useful for the cast member as it is for the guest. This can guarantee that none of the guest's time is being wasted while they are on their vacations.

Traditions is wrapped up with a trip to the Magic Kingdom (awesome, right?!) For cast members working at the Magic Kingdom they park in a place called West Clock. Then they board a bus which drives them to the backstage entrance for cast members. That's exactly what my Traditions group did as well. It was cool to see the backstage area of the theme park that started it all at Disney World, and for it to be on one of your first official days as a cast member is pretty special.

There's this story about Walt Disney that goes back to the early days of Disneyland. One day he was sitting on a park bench in Tomorrowland just watching the guests and cast members as he would often do. The cast member parking lot for Disneyland was directly behind Tomorrowland. In order to get to your location you'd have to walk through Tomorrowland to get there. As Walt was sitting there he saw a cast member in costume as a cowboy making his way to Frontierland for his shift. Ever the showman Walt was none too pleased to see this happen. A cowboy walking through an area themed to the future completely ruined the show. In that moment he knew that the next park he built would not have this problem.

The Utilidors (short for utility corridors) fixed that problem in the Magic Kingdom. When you walk into the park as a guest you're not actually on the ground floor. In fact you're ten feet above it. The Utilidors below act as an underground central highway for cast members. If you look at the Magic Kingdom from one of the resorts or from the Ticketing and Transportation Center, the lake in front of you, the Seven Seas Lagoon, is actually man made. It was excavated when Disney World was being built and the dirt taken from there was used to elevate the land where the Magic Kingdom would be. That's how the Utilidors were able to be created.

When you're on this bus during Traditions it drops you off right where the Utilidors begin. It's this huge entrance where cast members are constantly coming and going. The seemingly never ending, and confusing might I add, network of hallways can get you to almost any section of the park. You simply take a walk way, go to you destination, take the right stairwell up and then emerge backstage in one of the lands. It's really really cool but of course intimidating for new people. Luckily I thought to myself I wouldn't need to figure it out for my location (little did I know that five months later I would need to!).

Our Traditions facilitators led us through the maze and brought us up to certain areas in the park. Our mission once we were onstage was to keep an eye out for the Four Keys being used in real time. We'd look for cast members and see how they were practicing safety, being courtesy to a guest, keeping up with the show or maintaining efficiency. We walked around Fantasyland for a little and then headed out.

When we got back out facilitators said they had a surprise for us. The door opened and the big cheese himself showed up. He had a special gift for us too. Our nametags! It was quite the sight to finally be able to see my name on one of those bad boys. Traditions is just awesome, it's an incredible kickoff to training and a warm welcome to the company. Each class has two facilitators who are cast members themselves. You have to apply to be a facilitator and it's a rigorous application process. Only the very best cast members are able to become them. Your time as a Traditions facilitator only lasts for one year but it's definitely an awesome opportunity and they set an example of what great cast members should be.

After Traditions your next step in training depends on where you will be working. There can be a whole lot of different steps involved too. For Front Desk cast members you had a welcome class to working at resorts, then a welcome to Lodging class, then it gets more specific to your role.

Front desk is one of the more extensive training processes. It entails a lot of new software systems to learn, procedures, as well as a whole host of other topics you have to speak knowledgeably on. Once you get out of the "overview" classes at Disney University then you dive into a class called "Destination Cashier". Like the name suggests the class shows you the ins and outs of what it takes to be a "cashier". This term "cashier" is an important distinction because depending on your resort you can be a Front Desk cast member but still have different roles. One day you could be a cashier, the next you could work curbside check-in and you could even be a runner which has several different tasks. But more on those roles later!

Your first priority in Front Desk is learning what it takes to actually work the Front Desk as the cashier. You're called a cashier because you'll be processing payments when individuals check-in. As a cashier your main duty is facilitating check-ins/outs and while you have other tasks helping guests with the check-ins are the most important aspect.

Learning the processes involved to a check-in is no easy feat. In fact there are 11 steps you need to do in order for a proper Disney check-in to occur. Just learning that order and not forgetting a step can be a big challenge for many. On top of that you have to learn LILO which is the online reservation system Disney resorts use. This is the software cast members are looking at on their computer screens when they check you in, and yes it is LILO like from Lilo and Stitch. But like most things at Disney it is actually an acronym for Last In Last Out. Let me tell you something about LILO, she is a fickle system. A common phrase we would say almost daily was, "Oh LILO, she's moving slow today".

If you think about it though it really is an incredible system. There's something like 30,000 hotel rooms at Disney and LILO manages all of them. Not only that but it manages all hotel reservations. Since you can book nearly a year in advance LILO has to know all those reservations as well.

So it was quite the process to fully understand how to use LILO. Plus when I began my training Magic Bands were still in their infancy. This added another layer to the check-in process. You would need to make sure all the Magic Bands seemed to be working correctly before the check-in was complete. Just one more thing to take into consideration.

One of the harder things was actually learning how to count. Let me explain....

As a cashier you mainly would process credit cards for payments but occasionally you would need to do a cash payment. Each cast member would have a "bank" which is just a cash drawer in order to facilitate this process. Disney teaches you a very unique way of counting though. Let's say someone's total came to $1,001. They hand you $1,100 in cash and in order to give them change you would need to count up to $1,100. You start at $1,000 and then with each domination you give them you would say the next number. In this example you would need to give them $99 in change so it would be a $50, 2 $20, a $5 and four $1. Here's how that would go, "And $1,000 we have $50, $70, $90, $95 and four $1s make it $1,100." It might seem easy but it's a very confusing process to count up from where you start rather than just counting the change you own the guest.

I just watched the *Incredibles 2* at the time of writing this and there's a scene where Mr. Incredible is helping Dash with his math problem. Dash at one point says "Dad that's not how they taught us" at which point Mr. Incredible says, "We'll it's how I know how to do it, they can't just change math like that!". That's pretty much exactly how I felt. "Ok we know everyone here knows how to count but forget that because we're going to show you a new way." It was crazy! I would often find that it was confusing for the guests as well. Luckily, cash payments were not too frequent.

I actually really enjoyed the class overall though. My group had close to 20 people in it with most of them being college programmers in it. Several we're even going to be working at Yacht & Beach too. One would even turn out to be my roommate and a good friend later on! It was cool because you were able to develop a relationship with your fellow classmates as well as your instructors. For the most part we had the same instructors throughout the whole week. They would share their stories about working at the Front Desk or Concierge. I love that Disney lets the trainers be current cast members in your role. It's so much better than just hiring facilitators because the cast members who teach you have walked the walked which is incredibly valuable.

A part of Destination Cashier included a learning lab component. There was a small room filled with a line of computers. A couple days in we were able to go in there and run a couple practice check-ins. You would process a check-in while a fellow classmate pretended to be a guest and then you'd switch. It was cool to finally be able to go through the 11 step check-in process but I knew out in the real world it'd still be a challenge. Luckily I still had a lot more training to do!

Eventually your time comes and you're ready to move on. Destination Cashier is actually filled with Front Desk and Concierge cast members. From here Concierge cast members move on to do even more training at Disney University. They learn about dining reservations, ticket purchasing and a lot of other stuff they help guests facilitate.

The amount of time spent at Disney University was actually pretty crazy. All my roommates' roles were either in Quick Service Food & Beverage or Attractions. So they had their intro classes at Disney University and then immediately went to their role locations. Meanwhile I had close to two additional weeks at Disney University before I was able to head to my location. But at last my time had come! I was ready to head to the Yacht & Beach Club.

CHAPTER SIX

Welcome Aboard

But first more training. That's right, I finally made it out of Disney University but more training awaited me when I arrived at Yacht & Beach Club. The first day was called "Welcome Aboard" (getting it, cause it's a Yacht & Beach Club?) which was an orientation of the resort. Our facilitators came from several roles within the resort. They told us about the history of the Yacht & Beach Club, important amenities and then proceed to take us on a tour of the resort both onstage and backstage. We went all over the resort as there were many different roles represented in the class.

It was a nice introduction to the place where I'd be spending most of my time. It ended with us going to costuming and to get our clothes. Now costuming works differently at different places. Most resorts have their own costuming place backstage but some share it with another location. The parks all have their own so if you work in any role at the parks there's one main location you go to. Yacht & Beach Club had their own backstage right at the main cast member entrance. It was also right by the lockers and changing rooms which made it very convenient.

My outfit at the Front Desk wasn't bad at all. Gray pants, white shirt, silver and red striped tie and a bluish sport coat. The next time you go to Disney World take a look at the cast members you see. Admire their outfits and then ask yourself, "could I see myself wearing that or would I look ridiculous?" Chances are more often than not you would say "I'd look ridiculous". When you have a half decent costume you consider yourself very lucky.

Alright, I got my costume, I got my bearings of the resort, I got a couples weeks worth of training from Disney University. I'm ready for my first day by myself on the Front Desk!

Not so fast eager McBeaver, you've still got 5 more days with a trainer before you're by yourself.

Wait...what?

That's right the next five days at your resort are spent with a trainer stand right by you. The first couple of days you just observe how your trainer processes check-ins. Then you take the reigns as your trainer sits back and makes sure you're doing everything correctly.

Now you might be thinking this is a crazy amount of training and I was thinking the same thing around this time as well. But then I figured out why this was all necessary. The phrase, "first impressions are everything" really does ring true. As a Front Desk cast member you are often one of the first cast members a guest will interact with on their trip. You have to make a good first impression to ensure their trip gets off to a great start.

For many they are spending a lot of money on a trip to Disney World. You want to make sure that they enjoy every single aspect of it. There are a lot of small details that have to be handled during a check-in and they are all important to make sure everything goes well for the guest. You add their credit card so they can charge things to the room, you'll explain the Disney Dining Plan to them if they have it, you show them the layout of the resort, answer their questions and make sure they are all comfortable.

You are doing so much more than just telling them their room number. What you are actually doing is setting the guest up for a successful trip. Disney World is truly a World. It's massive and their are a lot of points where guests can get confused. When you have a smooth check-in you are guaranteeing they are getting off to a good start. If that first interaction is bad and problems occur that will leave a bad taste in their mouth. Disney wants them to have a great time and then come back in the future. That's why there is so much involved in the training.

In other roles like Attractions, Merchandise or Quick Service Food and Beverage, your interactions with guests can feel short and limited. As a Front Desk cast member you spend a solid amount of time with them and you often can see a guest several times during their stay. It's important that you set a good tone with them. Once I realized that that was what we were doing I understood why there was so much training involved.

I had two trainers over my five days and luckily for me they had the earliest shift possible! (sarcasm very much intended). I had to arrive at the resort every day at 5:45 a.m. You would get off around 2:45 p.m. every day but still getting up at that time was brutal. Luckily, those were really the only days I had to wake up that early. college programmers would often work the late shifts so I quickly got use to getting off at 11 p.m.

Throughout your training your trainer would basically quiz you on certain aspects of the role. The first day or so you would just sit back and watch them process check-ins and perform other tasks. But then by day three or so it was pretty much all on you. Your trainer would stand behind you to make sure you were doing everything correctly but they were more there as a safety net than anything else. Throughout that time your trainer has a checklist of things you have to master. As you show proficiency in each one your trainer would check off that you've got it down. By the last day each task should be marked off and after weeks of training you'd be ready to go at it alone.

Needless to say I was ready for that and FINALLY my time had come.

CHAPTER SEVEN

A Day in the Life of a Front-Desk Cast Member

Most days on the Front Desk were straightforward.

At Yacht & Beach the backstage area where cast members would enter was kind of in between the two lobbies of the resorts. You'd enter the building and the first thing you'd walk into was basically a cast member lounge. There were couches, a TV, some computers to check your emails and there were always cast members from all roles buzzing around. This was also where you'd find your locker, changing rooms and costuming.

This is typically where my shift would begin. If I needed a new costume I'd check one out. If I still had clean ones in my locker then I'd get what I needed and go change.

Once changed I would head over to wherever I was working that day. The HUB was the online intranet for Disney World and this is where you find your upcoming schedule, see cast member events and learn about cast member benefits and discounts among other things. When you work the Front Desk at Yacht & Beach your trained to work at both locations. Your schedule would reflect this with a simple YC for Yacht and BC for beach. Whatever was on my schedule that day is where I would head off to. Beach Club from the main backstage entrance was very close. Just a few yards away you would enter in the back office. (The back office is the name of the location directly behind the check-in area. This is actually where your call gets accepted if you were to call from your room. cast members back there are also placing reservations and assigning rooms to individuals.) The Yacht Club was a further walk however. One that would require you to walk outside and then enter into the main lobby of the resort. You'd walk into the lobby and then proceed into a door by check-in. This is where the back office for Yacht Club was.

Once it was time for your shift to officially start you would go to clock in. There were several clock-in/clock-out locations throughout the resort. These were simply just boxes on the wall where you would hit the clock in button and then swipe your company ID. It would process then tell you, you were all set.

As a cashier at Yacht & Beach your next step would be to get your cash drawer. Everyday in the back office you would see your name written on a whiteboard with the hours you were working and a number next to it. The number next to your name would signify what cash drawer you would need to get and what station you would be placed at while working the desk. So you'd find out what your number was and then collect the key to access your cash drawer.

All the keys to the cash draws as well as several master keys for the resort were stored in this metal and glass cabinet built into the wall. In order to unlock the cabinet you would have to swipe your company ID and then put in your perner number. The Perner number was just like your employee number, like a Social Security number you had for being a cast member. You'd type in the number of the key you need to get. The cabinet would unlock and then it would also unlock the hole of the key you needed to access as well. You grab the key, which was the only one you'd be able to take as everything else was still locked, and then close the cabinet to lock it back up.

This seems like quite the process but as each key can access a cash drawer with a lot of money and other keys could get you into any room in the resort, safety was of utmost priority. You'd also be able to see which employee had which keys out at anytime. You'd keep your keys for the day close to you as losing them would be a big deal.

A funny story about this. One time a co-worker of my forgot to lock his keys back up one day after his shift was done. He drove home only to get a call a few hours later from a manger saying his keys were missing. He reached into his pocket and discovered the keys he had forgotten to check back in. So he had to get back in his car, drive to Yacht & Beach and lock them up for the night.

Once you have your keys you walk over to a set of cubbies and unlock the one with your number on it. You'd count your cash drawer and this process varies from resort to resort. In each resort you'll count your money in the drawer and make sure it is all accounted for both in total and in denominations (the right amount of $20s, $10s, $5s, etc). Where it changes from resort to resort is the amount each draw contains. It really is on a case-by-case basis but the Deluxe resorts would have cash drawers with more money in it than the cash drawers of a Moderate or Value resort typically. Since the rooms themselves are more expensive at a Deluxe, that might require you to make bigger amounts of change.

After your cash drawer was all squared away you would then login to the reservation system LILO and "Bank In". This basically means, you have arrived for work, your cash draw is all in order and you are ready to start your day. You'll take your cash draw then walk on stage to the station with the number you were assigned at the start of your shift. By station I simply mean the computer that you will be working on that day. You'll log into LILO on that computer and then start your shift!

The biggest and most frequent task was checking guests in. You'd always be able to tell if it was going to be a busy or slow day based on the amount of check-ins. In the top corner of LILO it would tell you the total amount of check-ins and how many there were left for that day at your resort. Whether you were at the Yacht Club or the Beach Club, if you would ever see that number and it was above something like 300 check-ins you knew it was going to be a very busy day. Which is funny because if there were only 300 check-ins for the day at a place like an All-Star Resort they would think there was something wrong. A crazy busy day at Yacht & Beach Club would be a light day at the larger resorts.

May God have mercy on those cast members who have to process that amount of check-ins everyday!

The more and more I did it the more I grew to love the check-in process. As I progressed I was able to formulate a spiel that I would do. It was almost like I was doing a performance with every check-in I completed. I also loved check-ins because it was a way to have an elongated conversation with guests. One thing that I was looking forward to the most when it came to working at Disney was being able to share my love and knowledge of the place. Anytime I was able to assist people with their questions about the parks or resorts was always a fun time for me. During check-in this was always the best chance of doing that.

Check-outs were fairly easy. I would let the guest know of any outstanding charges that would be processed with their credit card on file. I would give them a receipt if they wanted one and help them with any last minute requests. These were much less time consuming than check-ins.

Other tasks were really up to the guest. Meaning it was more just answering any questions they had. I would see if I could get them a late check-out, give them tips about the resort, print out the amount of dining credits they had left on their dining plan or maybe paying their balance down with Disney gift cards rather than the credit card they had on file. If they ever had any concerns about their rooms or wanted to move I would see if I could accommodate that. We were also like the complaint desk of the hotel so I would have to listen to their issues as they complained to me. I never really liked that part mostly just because it was awkward and many times there were rarely things I could do. Requests like "I want a room with a fireworks view" were just unable to be accommodated as there weren't really any rooms at the resort that were ideal for Illuminations viewing. That was always hard to explain and guests would get frustrated with the answer.

But you would have to just smile through it and move on.

Other than that your day might consist of your manager having you run to a room to give something to a guest or complete another task.

As a cashier you would get one hour-long break that occurred about half-way through your shift. Typically at this point I'd go to the staff cafeteria. Located in the backstage area by Costuming, the staff cafeteria, called the Jib and Jaw (Jib for short), was where most would go on their breaks as well. They had grab and go selections and made to order food as well but I would only indulge in that every once and awhile when I would forget to bring something. It wasn't world class food but it would get the job done.

Breaks were always fun because you got to sit with your co-workers both from the Yacht Club and the Beach Club. It was kind of funny because in a lot of ways the Jib was like your cafeteria back in High School. Each role sat with each other and rarely mingled. The Front Desk and concierge cast members sat in one spot, lifeguards sat in another and merchandise sat elsewhere. There weren't any rules to it, it just seemed to work out that way. But it makes sense. You would sit with the people you knew the best and those were your role co-workers.

After your break it was back to the Front Desk for the second half of your shift. More of the same until your "bank out" time came. This would typically occur thirty minutes before your actual clock-out time. This was the case because you would have to "bank out" or add up your cash drawer to make sure it was all accounted for.

Throughout your shift you would keep track of all the payments you took. On a special piece of paper you would write the reservation number, the amount of the payment and then how that payment was processed (credit card, cash, check). LILO would keep track as well but this was just a way for you to double check to make sure everything was all there. When you would count your cash drawer at the end of your shift you would also add up the total payments you processed and then bank out. In LILO you would make sure the numbers were all the same. If it was you'd click end and your shift was just about done. If the numbers didn't match you'd need to figure out where it went wrong. Usually it would be you forgot to write something down or your clicked credit card instead of cash while you were checking someone in.

After that you'd lock your cash drawer up in the cubbie you got it from and then lock your keys back up. Most days all your transactions would be done by credit card. But some days you would collect a cash payment, or worse a check! If you took a cash payment you would need to deposit that. This would require you to do some additional paperwork, put the money in a special bag that could be locked and then you would have to walk to where all the cash was deposited in the resort. You were required to walk there with a co-worker as well since you had cash on you. You'd deposit the cash in a big money counter and then that was typically it. You'd drop the bag back off and call it a day.

Now you can see why this role has so much training involved with it. Nothing is crazy complicated, the processes just have many separate steps involved. Missing one step could mean having to spend a lot of time fixing it. Since you were dealing with large amounts of cash Disney always wanted to make sure it was being handled correctly.

Going into the cash room was always an eye opening experience. For starters you had in your mind how much you had taken in payments for the day. Typically it could be well over $10,000 depending on how many check-ins you did and how expensive their rooms were. Every once and awhile you'd see Merchandise cast members deposited cash from the retail locations. That was always quite a sum of cash as well. Then you'd start thinking. I am just one person at one resort on Disney property taking in this amount of money in one day. You'd consider all the other resorts, all the stores, restaurants in every hotel and park and all of a sudden you realize just how much money is coming in every single day. It's crazy!

Once you come to it after your existential crisis surrounding how much money there is, it was your time to clock out! Process was relatively the same as clock-in, only difference is on the time clock you would hit "clock out" and then swipe your card. Once you started getting familiar with your cash counting process you were able to complete it in five to ten minutes. Since you would begin your bank out thirty minutes before you actually clocked out you would typically have time to just hang out. Which was always great to decompress before you left for the day.

While there was never really a completely typical day, you'd always run into challenges, the days would sometimes run together. But the Front Desk was just the first position you would learn.

CHAPTER EIGHT

Coming Out From Behind the Desk

I loved working the Front Desk. But as the days started running together the mundane began to set in. There was a way to relive this however. Depending on what resort you worked out you were able to learn different positions within Front Desk. It might seem a little confusing since the role name is Front Desk, but the other positions work hand-in-hand.

The two other positions you could be trained on as a Front Desk cast member at Yacht & Beach were called runner and curbside. I was never trained as a runner but as the name implies you would basically "run" around performing various tasks. These tasks would include delivering items to rooms and even checking rooms to make sure they were in proper order. Sometimes there were discrepancies within LILO. Like it would say a guest is checking into an occupied room. No real rhyme or reason for this but it would require a runner to go to the room to double check. Every once and awhile a runner would have to actually drive somewhere else to retrieve something. It could be getting a bag a guest left somewhere or maybe event creating a magical moment. They might go to Magic Kingdom's backstage and get character autographs for a child who was having a hard time or something like that. A runner definitely never had two identical days.

I was however trained as a curbside cast member. This entailed me working outside on the "curb" of course. Years before I had arrived Disney had rolled out their online check-in process. This allowed guests to check-in ahead of when they arrive in order to spend up the check-in process. With the dawn of My Disney Experience and your room key being sent to you in the form of a Magic Band before you arrived, for many you were able to bypass the Front Desk all together. As curbside cast members our job was to welcome individuals to the resort. We were armed with iPads equipped with LILO on them so we were able to greet arriving guests and look them up to see if they were already checked in or still needed to go to the Front Desk.

This was a way to alleviate wait times at the Front Desk and make the check-in process quicker for guests who had utilized online check-in. It was also a great first touch point. But there was another layer to it. Guests would typically arrive either by Disney's Magical Express which was available to all guests staying at a Disney owned resort. The Magical Express transports you from Orlando International Airport to the Disney resort you're staying at. As you enter the Magical Express bus you were "scanned on". When each bus would leave the airport curbside cast members were able to see who was going to be on the next bus. This was an awesome way for us to "surprise" guests when they arrived since we were able to greet them by name. You would be able to see how many people were in the party and then from that you could determine which party was which. Sometimes you just had to guess but it was still neat for the guests.

An exchange of this would go as such:

- A party gets off the bus
- I greet them by saying, "Hello, is this the Brown party?"
- Shocked the guest would respond, "Yes! But how did you know?"
- I would proclaim, "Well my friend Mickey told me you were coming and he wanted me to make sure I welcomed you when you arrived."

This is one of the reasons I began to prefer curbside over the actual Front Desk. I never grew tired of seeing guests reactions as I would welcome them by name. It was a perfect way of welcoming them and starting their vacation off right.

The second way of arriving was of course by car. Everyday a list of each party checking in would be created with each party being assigned a number from one to whatever the amount of check-ins were there for the day. Each curbside cast member had access to this list as well as the Security Guards at the Resort's Welcome Gate. Each guest arriving would be required to present photo ID and then say they were checking in. The Security Guard would see the ID and find the number of the reservation it corresponded with. Once he waved them through he would get on the walkie talkie and announce what number guest was arriving and the make, model and color of the car they were in. Each curbside cast member (equipped with a walkie talkie) would find the number then look them up in LILO and be able to welcome them by name when they exited their vehicle.

People were always just amazed by this. They loved this little piece of magic and I loved to be apart of that little magic. Working curbside made those moments occur because you captured guests right in their first moments arriving at the resort and on

Disney property. The excitement levels for everyone are always incredibly high at this time. In this moment you got to experience that with the guests, their excitement always made you smile.

This was also a great time to interact with guests to see what they have planned for their trip. You can ask them what rides they plan on riding and give them tips about the resort or the parks. Since curbside cast members were stationed by the front door of the resort you would see everyone as they came in from the buses. Which meant once you checked someone in there was a good chance you'd be seeing them again sometime during their stay.

Really, this is all I ever wanted to do when it came to working at Disney World. I had bigger plans and aspirations for working for Disney but I came into my college program with the idea of "giving back". I had been to Disney World so many times before my program started that I already knew the place like the back of my hand. Some would say I was even obsessed with the place (which is most likely pretty accurate). I'd come to realize that my trips had been incredible because of the cast members making everything work. You'd also remember specific cast members from past trips. That's what I wanted to do, share thoughts and tips with guests just like previous cast members had done for me. Working curbside made occur more often than working Front Desk.

I also enjoyed curbside because it allowed you to hand guests off. Like I said before my least favorite part of the Front Desk was handling angry guests. I enjoyed solving problems but when it came to guests voicing their anger at me, I was never the best at handling and processing that. That never occured working curbside. If a guest has a discrepancy I was very limited in what I could do since I only had an iPad to work with. Because of this I would need to hand off the guest to a fellow cast member working the Front Desk if an issue required greater attention. I know this might seem a little petty but when you're working long days these little things can really help you out.

A second duty when working curbside included making sure to capture VIP and Club Level guests. At the deluxe resorts there is a floor designated as Club Level. What this means is that you get a little more personalized attention. Only those staying on that level could get there and outside the elevator there were always a couple Concierge cast members that would check you in and facilitate any requests you had during your stay. The main appeal of staying Club Level was access to the Club Level Lounge. Here you would be able to grab complimentary food and beverages. Depending on the time of day the lounge would have breakfast, snacks, hors d'oeuvres and desserts. Plus you could also get beer and wine.

In order to make the biggest impact what we would do on curbside is escort the guests up to the Club Level to check-in and make sure they were all settled. It was just part of that Disney touch that showed how we would go above and beyond for the guests. It would work the same way for VIPs as well. A VIP can be a celebrity, an important guest or even an important Disney employee. VIP didn't mean they would be automatically staying on Club Level but it did mean we would need to get a Manager and do a meet and greet. Just another little touch.

The roles associated with Front Desk vary from resort to resort. Not every resort has a curbside cast member and in fact as I was heading into my second program that position was greatly being cut across property. So it was a case by case basis depending on the resort you're at. It's interesting because while all these resorts are under one company in Disney they all operated differently. Not vastly different but little things here and there would be done differently. It makes sense since these resorts have sometimes over 1,000 employees. They were handled like their own individual organizations.

As an example the position of runner was drastically different at Caribbean Beach resort when compared to Yacht & Beach. I was once talking to a cast member who had worked there and he was saying how the runner there basically drove a van around all day because the resort was so large.

When you work at Disney you discover that Full Time cast members seem to change roles and locations a lot. Since there were so many different places to work and they all operated so differently it is just a way to get a change of pace. The work can be monotonous and any change of pace you can get is a welcome site. Having the opportunity to learn these new positions while being a part of the Front Desk was an awesome opportunity and when compared to roles my roommates had, it was also a rare occurrence.

CHAPTER NINE

A Note on Costumes and Costuming

Each role at Disney World has its own unique costume like I explained earlier. Mine for the Front Desk wasn't too bad. Each location has its own costuming location where you go to pick up new costumes. The parks all had their own buildings usually backstage or in the parking lots. These places were massive obviously because it held costumes for every role in a park and it had to have enough sizes and quantities to accommodates the 1,000s of cast members that worked there.

Resorts were a little different. While most resorts were massive and had hundreds if not thousands of employees working there, some were of course larger than others. Because of this your costuming location varied from resort to resort. Places like the All-Star Resorts all shared one Costuming location. Because of this the building that housed all the costumes wasn't located in any one resorts in particular. Some might be located in completely separate places away from process resort.

Luckily for me the Yacht & Beach Clubs' Costuming was located in the cast member lounge as you first entered the building. If I needed fresh costumes I'd walk into Costuming and get them. Before you leave you would have to check-out the items. Which kind of works the same way as you would check-out a book from the library. You'd go up to a monitor, scan your employee ID then each piece of clothing had a barcode which you would also scan. You'd click done and go about your merry way. The process was kind of the same whenever you would need to return something. It would be placed in a bin where it was scanned as checked back in.

Later on when I would work at the Mine Train the process was pretty much the same but there were a few differences. Costuming itself was located in the cast parking lot behind the Magic Kingdom itself. This building was absolutely massive! You would walk in and it looked like the scene at the end of Indiana Jones and the Raiders of the Lost Ark when the government is putting the Ark of the Covenant in the warehouse, the camera pans up and the building just keeps going forever and ever. This was kind of like that but with the added element that you as the cast member had to find something. Now during training they would show you were to go but it can still get confusing.

The building is segmented by lands so for the Mine Train I would walk to the far right and head to the Fantasyland section. Here I would be able to get the basics of my costume. The pants and the shirt. But for your accessory pieces like the belt with satchel I was required to wear, those were located kind of in the middle of the Costuming building. There was also optional long white socks and a hat you could wear. I did not indulge in either of those. Having to wear the required pieces was already a little embarrassing so I had to save some of my dignity, right?! So the stocking like white socks and farmer's hat did not make the cut for me.

Once you have all the pieces you needed you'd go to check-out. Now this was a little different compared to Yacht & Beach because it was always crowded.

You would lineup much you would do at a Target or Marshalls. When it was your turn you'd scan your ID and then just sort of wave your items in front of the computer and it would be able to account for all of them. Well most of them, it didn't work too too well. But for the most part it was fine.

The big difference for me when comparing costuming at Yacht & Beach to Magic Kingdom revolved around logistics. At Yacht & Beach I'd show up like fifteen minutes before my shift, get a new costume and then go right into the locker room a few feet away and get changed into it. At Magic Kingdom I would typically arrive to work in my Costume. When you park in the cast lot you would have to take the West Clock bus which actually takes you into the Magic Kingdom. I would take the bus and get off at the first stop where New Fantasyland and Storybook Circus was. If I was to go one more stop then I would arrive at the main entrance to the Utilidors. This is where the locker rooms were located.

For me to get my costume at Costuming, take the bus one stop further, go to the locker rooms, change, get back on the bus or walk to the other backstage entrance and then walk to the Mine Train would just be adding so much time to the process. Since I would typically get off very late Costuming would most likely be closed by the time I left the park. Which meant picking up a new Costume usually occurred during an off day. Not ideal in my book but that's the way it worked out. That's just one example of how being only four miles apart actually felt world's apart when you worked at Disney.

This Costuming process seemed simple and it was for the cast member checking out the costume but, what was required on the backend had to just be a massive computer system. Everytime you would check something in or out you would see a list of every costume piece that should have currently been in your possession. Imagine keeping track of that for every single costumed cast member (manager level and above didn't wear costumed clothes). That's tens of thousands of individuals to keep information on.

I smile just thinking of it because these features were always what made me so excited to learn when I became a cast member. You can learn all about the history of the parks, you can memorize everything that is offered there and formulate your own personal tips and tricks but there is so much you will never know until you actually work there. The little things like how costumes work and the infrastructure needed to keep it all running was what fascinated me.

A couple tips on Costuming if you ever plan on working at Disney. They won't provide shoes for you in most instances. Rather than buying before you start work, wait until you first day of backstage training. Ask your training leader what the shoe requirements are and if they have any recommendations. Since you don't know where you will be working on the college program until you get there you wouldn't want to buy a pair of shoes that would end up not working for you. Whatever selection you make be sure they are comfortable as you will be doing a lot of standing and walking in most roles.

While there are probably hundreds of thousands of individual costume pieces it won't always be easy to find pieces that fit you. One of my co-workers was the same size as me at Yacht & Beach. He and I would always have trouble finding the size that fit us best. It basically came to, if I knew the size I wanted wasn't there then he probably had it checked out and vice versa. You can totally take your costume home and wash it yourself to prevent this though. If you have a piece that fits perfectly and you don't want to get rid of it, hold on to it! Wash it yourself and keep it for as long as you want.

You'll definitely want to keep track of everything though. If you were to change roles or leave the company with something being checked out they would end up charging you for the item. It's not totally expensive but you don't want that to happen especially as it is easily preventable.

Costuming is easy once you get the hang of it and it a fascinating process that just makes you appreciate Disney World more and more once you become a cast member.

CHAPTER TEN

My Grand Plan

I had a grand plan in my mind of what I was going to do and who I was going to be after I graduated college. It took different shapes throughout the years but the core of it always remained the same. I was going to work at Disney.

Early on in my life I remember, like many Disney fans, wanting to be an Imagineer. I was always so fascinated with the parks, the attractions that comprised them and the details that made them stand out from other rides and parks I had been to. Once I realized that the people who created these attractions had a specific name, I knew I had to learn anything and everything I could about them. I became enthralled with knowing who the Imagineers were, what their process was and how they came to build these iconic attractions I had grown to love.

Learning as much as I could about the history of the parks was how I was able to fill the Disney void in my heart in between my trips. Anything I could get my hands on when it came to the parks I would consume. Books, TV shows, blog posts, ideas, podcasts. I would find anything I could just to learn more about the history of my favorite place on Earth. Each story I would learn almost always revolved around some of the Imagineers themselves. Since they were the ones that were thinking up these ideas and then also designing and creating them, their stories were always incredibly captivating.

The more stories I learned the more I kept seeing the same names come up more and more. People like Marc Davis, Alice Davis, Marty Sklar, X Atencio, Mary Blair, Tony Baxter and Joe Rhode. These were the people that built the parks and the classic rides like Haunted Mansion, Pirates of the Caribbean, Big Thunder Mountain Railroad and Splash Mountain. It was incredible to learn about these and other Imagineers because you put these attractions on a pedestal. How could any human come up and formulate these ideas from blank page to constructed attraction? Yet here they were. Normal people coming up with extraordinary ideas.

I knew I had to be one of these people. I just had to be an Imagineer. I would come up with attractions of my own complete with stories and names for them as well. I was going to try my best to be one of these incredible people. The more I learned the more I realized I probably wasn't going to get the chance though unfortunately. While I definitely had the imagination I knew I probably didn't have the engineering skills to round out the Imagineering term. I'm just awful at math, physics, etc. I knew that engineering was not in my future. I discovered that it wasn't just engineers at Imagineering. There were painters, sculptures and designers that were also considered Imagineers. Which would be great if I had any artistic abilities but, alas I do not! I was slowly coming to realize that maybe Imagineering probably just wasn't for me.

I know that it's a huge division within the Disney company and there are plenty of roles outside of engineering or being an artist. They have their accountants, their construction leads, thier project managers. I could've tried to get in via one of those avenues but if

I was going to be working at Imagineering I wanted to be able to make the attractions. Not just sit close by while all that was going on. I needed a different direction.

My new plan was to work for Disney in a department that I would enjoy. A department and a position that I would be happy to work in or outside of Disney. I didn't know just what that was going to be but I figured I could find that out in college. I had always known of the Disney College Program and I figured that, that would be my way to put my foot in the door. But as I started researching more and more I would come to find there was another avenue open for college students. That avenue was something called Disney Professional Internships.

While the college program is focused more on the front-line duties of working in the parks, the professional internships are more geared toward corporate jobs. Working in lines of business that might be incorporated in the parks but didn't necessarily work in the parks themselves. They also had professional internships at other Disney businesses like the movie studios, ABC, ESPN, etc. But I was most focused on the park based ones.

So that was my plan. Work in the parks, have fun on my off days as I explored Orlando. Get a professional internship then work my way up from there. It was a perfect plan and was going to make for a great story as I rose through the company ranks. It was also a plan had by thousands of other college students beside me.

When I was in college I knew I wanted to study abroad for a semester. Traveling has always been a big part of my life. I think it's very beneficial and learning about new cultures is always a good thing. Having the opportunity to live in a foreign country for several months was something very appealing to me. It was something I knew I might never be able to do again after I graduated college. So that became part of my plan.

This made things a little more complicated as I've stated before. Since I was studying abroad I really only had one opportunity to get my action plan right. I needed to get into the college program for the summer or fall immediately following my graduation. Then from there I would have to apply to professional internships as I was down working in Orlando in hopes of getting into one following my college program. This is important because you can't apply to professional internships or the college program if you are more than six months out of college. So basically I had one shot at making my grand plan come true.

As you now know I was able to complete step one of my grand plan. I got into the college program immediately following my college graduation. By this point I knew what line of business I wanted to go into. In school I studied Communications and I had fallen in love with what I was learning. Things like advertising, social media and marketing were places where I could flex my creative muscles while not having to perform technical assignments. I loved being creative but I had struggled to find careers that allowed that where you weren't an artist or designer. When I started to realize that Communications incorporated these creative occupations in Marketing and Advertising I knew I found my calling.

I wanted to use my degree in Communications so during my first college program I began looking for professional internships in Marketing, Advertising, Social Media and the likes that revolved around the park's line of business. As I started looking I noticed there were a plethora of these internships available to apply to. I was beyond excited so I began submitting my application to ones that fit the framework of what I was looking for.

Over the course of the next couple of months I began to hear back from them. Or rather I began to not hear back from them. When you apply for the college program or professional internship you have an online portal where you're able to check the status of your application. A few weeks after I submitted my first application I went on there and noticed one of them said something to the effect of I was no longer in consideration for that role. "No big deal", I thought. I had plenty of others I was still in consideration for. Then I was no longer in consideration for another role. And then another. And another. Then all of a sudden I was no longer in consideration for any of them.

Needless to say, I was pretty devastated.

I knew my strategy of only giving myself one shot was a bit of a gamble but I at least thought I'd make it to the interview stage in one. If I could get the opportunity to plead my case I was sure I'd have a great chance of getting one of the roles. But alas, it never even came to that.

It's one of those life sequences where you begin to question everything you had done up until that point. Quite the life crisis to have at twenty-three! It was more than just not getting a job though. It was a lifetime of hopes and dreams just kind of ending. What sucked the most is knowing that I wanted to work for this company more than anything but I just didn't stand out enough when compared to others. There was nothing I could really do about it but that didn't ever stop me from thinking "what if?". What if I didn't study abroad and instead went to Disney then and came back later, what if I got a degree in something else, what if I tried for other roles. I knew that thinking wouldn't change anything but it might have helped as I coped with my new reality.

This is kind of common to experience in the college program as well. You'll see friends who don't get internships as well and who are devastated once it happens. What's really happening is you have a bunch of college kids who are unsure of their futures. When you put a lot of them together they can kind of egg each other on. Not to say it's right for them to complain, it's not. What happens is that while your whole future is ahead of you, it seems like nothing is actually out there for you. Being in a period of change can scare someone a lot, and it brews anxiety on top of that.

I don't want to seem like it was a miserable experience. Far from it! Just as I was living my life in Orlando, working in the parks I always had a voice in the back of my head saying "ok but, what's next?".

What was next for me? I had accomplished a whopping one-third of my grand plan and with the other sixty-six percent looking like they were not going to happen I had some unanswered questions I needed to figure out. I liked living in Orlando and I loved being at Disney. While I was denied by professional internships I wasn't ready to end my time in Florida just yet.

CHAPTER ELEVEN

Should I Stay or Should I Go

college programs are split up by semester. The Fall program will typically take you from August until early January. The Spring program will take you from January to early May. Spring Advantage will include the summer, meaning it starts in January and goes through August. Fall Advantage will work the other way having you start in May and end in January." through August and Fall Advantage will work the other way having you start in May. While these programs are only scheduled to last from five to eight months you are able to work for twelve consecutive months on the college program. Once your twelve months hits you can't go any further.

If you have yet to finish college you can go back for a semester or longer and then come back for another college program later. I know plenty of people who did multiple college programs spread out. It's not uncommon for some to do a college program in Disney World and then also do one out in California at Disneyland. It's also common for people to sign up for a regular program and then extend into the next program. Basically meaning you sign up for an additional program. Some would even extend into an Advantage period as well. For example I knew people who started in the Fall 2015 Program then come January they extended into the Spring 2016 program and then come May they extended into the Advantage 2016 program carrying them through August. Now you can't do a stand alone Advantage program. Sometimes they have an alumni only Summer program but for the most part you have to have another program attached to your Advantage session.

Extensions aren't always guaranteed. Disney typically decides halfway through the current program if they are going to open up extensions. That being said I can't recall ever hearing that Disney opted out of offering extensions for a program. They need the bodies to fill positions.

I got an email around October of my program saying extensions would open up for the Spring Program in a few weeks. Originally I decided to apply for an extension as a back up plan in case I didn't get a professional internship. I was happy I did too when I found out a professional internship wouldn't be in my future. As an important point you aren't guaranteed that you will be accepted if you apply for an extension. While you got in the first time doesn't mean you will be accepted a second. Now your record comes into play. If there are marks against you Disney can easily decide not to continue their relationship with you.

For me I had a clean record and was accepted into the program. Now to be fair when I was accepted I wasn't 100% sure I was going to stay down there. It was still up in the air for me. I loved my first program but I knew my roommates would be leaving and a lot of my current co-workers would be leaving too. Plus I found out that I'd be at a new location.

When you apply for an extension you are able to list where you would like to go or rather what roles you would like to extend to. You list them in order of preference and you are also given the option of selecting the same role at the same location or the same role at a new location. Disney does this just if you like where you are at and what to continue to work there or if you like your role and just what some new scenery. I had these listed as some of my top options but I decided to go a new route entirely. My number one option was being placed in attractions and my number two option was being placed in PhotoPass.

I can honestly say I didn't know why I selected these two over my current role as Front Desk at Yacht & Beach Club but I do know I always considered extending a backup plan. Because of this I am sure I just decided to change it up completely. When I was accepted I found out I was in attractions but they didn't tell me what park I would be in or what attraction I'd be at. This became another thing I had to consider when it came to accepting my extension or not. I could get placed on some awesome attractions but I could also be placed at some really bad attractions as well. I remember at one point going park by park and seeing which attractions I'd like to be at and which ones I would hate working at.

The time finally came and I had to decide if I was going to stay or not. What it came down to was realizing that an extra five months wasn't really that long in the grand scheme of things. Especially if you consider that this was probably going to be my last chances of working at Disney. Plus, I wanted to see if any new doors could open for me in that time. So it was settled, I was going to reup for one more run.

There was still that little question of finding where I was going to be working. I had always said I would have hated working on "it's a small world". So that was the one I really wanted to make sure I did not get placed at. At some point I found out that I would be working at the Magic Kingdom. Then I had a trainer from Yacht & Beach come up to me to give me my first week schedule at the Magic Kingdom and then I found out that I'd be placed in Fantasyland. "Dear lord", I thought to myself, "I'm actually going to get placed at 'it's a small world'". I was quickly considering everything.

One day during my final weeks a Yacht & Beach cast member friend came up to me and said he could probably figure out where I was going to be working. He was a trainer himself and there's one portal every trainer at Disney World can get into. Here is where all the training schedules are available. He looked my name up and I found out that I'd be working at....the Seven Dwarfs Mine Train.

A weight was lifted off my shoulders. I wouldn't be working at "it's a small world", huzah! Now I have no idea why I didn't want to work there so badly I just knew I didn't. So I was excited with my Seven Dwarfs Mine Train placement. Then I decided to open up the My Disney Experience app to check the wait time of the ride. I knew it was popular but I never put into context what it would be like to work there. I saw the wait time of well over two hours and I thought, "what have I gotten myself into?!?"

CHAPTER TWELVE

The Transition

In many ways extending your program can be like starting from scratch all over again. Sure you could get an extension at your same location. If that happens you don't have to go through training again, the only difference is really saying goodbye to current college programmers you worked with and saying hello to the new ones you'll be working with.

Even if that's the case you will still have some new things to conquer. To stay in your same apartment a certain percentage of your roommates must be staying as well. Usually, you'll be the lone wolf when it comes to extending. Obviously the fewer roommates you have the more likelihood that everyone will stay but a lot of the time you'll be the only one.

If this is the case then you'll be packing up your room and moving to a new location. I was able to select who I wanted to live with just like I was able to do at the start of my first program. Once I knew all my roommates were heading back home, I started seeing who was extending at work. Luckily one other guy was as well. We both agreed to live together and later on we would find out that we were indeed put in the same room. Which was awesome because he's an awesome guy and became one of my best friends during the college program.

The moving day process is very similar to your original arrival day. You show up bright and early at Vista

Way. There you head over to one of the clubhouses and proceed to check-in. There is a little bit of paperwork to do but then you find out your new apartment number and complex location. You get the key and it's off to explore your new digs.

For this program I decided to change it up a little housing complex wise. I liked Vista Way but I also knew it wouldn't hurt to try and get into something a little nicer. I didn't want to break the bank but I was also comfortable with the amount of roommates I was living with. So I was able to get my first location. A three bedroom unit in Chatham Square. Chatham was the second oldest complex behind Vista Way. While it's not as nice as The Commons or Paterson Court it's definitely an upgrade over Vista. At first the complex was a little confusing to navigate but I got use to it pretty quickly. My apartment was on the first floor and in one of the closet buildings to the front gate.

Now it hadn't been guaranteed or confirmed at this point that I was going to be living with the person I requested. So it was still up in the air. Once I got the key to my new place I dig a little final packing at Vista and drove over to Chatham. As I pulled into the complex there walking on the sidewalk was the guy I had requested to room with. Signs were looking good! As I parked and walked towards my apartment we saw each other and instantly became excited when we realized we were headed to the same unit. We entered the apartment and noticed a couple of people had already arrived. We took an empty room in the very back and were pretty excited that we were going to be living together for the next few months.

The rest of that first day covers your standing moving day stuff. I helped my roommate drive back to his old apartment, since he didn't have a car, and we brought over the rest of his stuff. We headed to the grocery store and made a couple other stops along the way. Moving days are always exhausting so the day didn't really last much longer than that.

As this was going on I had already begun training for my new location at Disney University. In fact there were a few days I spent completely alone in the three bedroom Vista Way apartment before my moving day came. Those days were a little lonely. Mostly because I was saying goodbye to fellow co-workers, roommates and other friends from my first program and then I would go back to my empty apartment. Not the greatest feeling in the world but such is life and that's how the program goes.

Training at Disney University for Attractions was much less intense when compared to Front Desk training. It was more broad and contained a lot of overviews. Training at Disney University itself lasted about two seminars or two days (I think some can have these seminars scheduled on different days). You start with "Welcome to Operations". You'll take part in this class with many different roles and the basic premise discusses safety and the Four Keys. This class lasts about 3 hours and after you typically have a second class to go to that day.

With your second class you get split depending on what role you have. I went to "Welcome to Park Operations". This was mainly for Attractions, Custodial and Park Greeter roles. Again just an overview to what these roles will entail and what will be common for you to see in the parks. Your instructors are always current cast members working in these roles. It's always cool to get their insights into the jobs and their stories help to keep the class a little livelier. All in all the training at Disney University was much less intense than my previous experiences and these classes really just ease you into the role.

As you complete your time at Disney University your next "work" day will be one of several orientation days. Since I was going to be in Magic Kingdom my first stop was "Once Upon a Time....Is Now!" (As an aside all the park orientation days have clever names. Animal Kingdom is often called DAK by cast members since it's Disney's Animal Kingdom, and their orientation is called "DAKlimation". EPCOT's is called "Discovery Day" since the park is all about discovering and exploring. Hollywood Studios' is called "On With the Show!") These orientations are a way to get cast members from all roles acclimated to the park. The day begins bright and early in the Utilidors under the Magic Kingdom. Aside from Traditions, this was going to be my first experience with navigating the underground tunnel system. I was a little nervous because they can seem daunting, and I'll be the first to admit that I never truly mastered them. But you are required to meet in the cast cafeteria affectionately named the "Mouseketeria".

Luckily it's pretty much impossible to get lost going to this place. You first park at the West Clock lot and then take the bus into the Magic Kingdom. That bus drops you at the entrance of the Utilidors and the "Mouseketeria" is one of the first things that you see. The Utilidors basically look like an entrance to a cave. Above it you can see Beast's Castle. There's also a wall of buildings and windows (those first windows you see are some of the management offices for Fantasyland attractions). Then below all that a dark tunnel begins. The tunnel is quite large I should say, so it's not actually scary. But it's still an interesting site to see and really not one you'd probably ever see before.

When you get off the bus you walk a few yards and enter the Utilidors where you stay towards the right side of the hall almost hugging the wall. There are painted lines basically ensuring that you stick to this path too. Reason being is that to your left vehicles are constantly whizzing by. Mostly they are the size of golf carts or a little bigger but still, best not to walk in that area. It's a site to see for many reasons. It's hard enough to fathom being underneath the most popular theme park in the world let alone being in an underground city essentially. One that is big enough to have vehicles traveling all around it.

One of the first places you see on your right is the Mouseketeria. It's your typical cafeteria with pretty much standard food selections. Pizza, burgers, salad bar and there was even a Subway in it. I had arrived around 6:30 a.m. or so and slowly the rest of the group participating in the orientation would arrive. There were probably upwards of 35 of us. We met our facilitators and we each got an ear piece to wear so that the facilitators could talk into a lapel mic and not have to raise their voice for us.

"Once Upon a Time...Is Now", is more or less a walking tour of the Magic Kingdom. Sure you learn about where the first aid stations are and where one might be able to find a drinking fountain (hint: there is always a drinking fountain by any bathroom). But overall it consisted of walking throughout the lands and hearing the history of the park and the attractions. At certain points you would also observe the guests and see how they interact with different things. It was also very cool to be standing on Main Street before really anyone else was in the park.

This orientation only lasts for about half the day. You get lunch in the Mouseketeria and then the group reforms and heads off to a training room. At this point you're really just following the crowd through the Utilidors. It didn't occur to me until a facilitator mentioned it but the training room we were in was in a bank of offices right above Main Street. I once heard

Dan Cockerell, who was the Vice President of Magic Kingdom, when I worked there describing his office above Main Street. How cool must that be? Everyday you go to your "office" and you can hear the parade and the guests below.

At this point more trainers enter the room and the group is broken off based upon their locations within the park. I had two trainers and about nine or so trainees in my group. We departed for our Fantasyland orientation. The trainers were awesome. They were super funny and welcomed us warmly. Both of the trainers I had were in attractions but several of the trainees with me had other roles. Which made sense since this was more a way for you to get your bearings set in Fantasyland.

We walked all over the place. Stopping at each store, restaurant, and attraction to discuss a little about it. Our trainers would explain what backstage entrances lead where and what ones were used to get to break rooms. We also learned some fun facts about the land so that we could entertain guests with them later. Our trainers got the sense we were still a little nervous about navigating the Utilidors so they gave us a brief tour of them as well.

Last stop on the orientation was costuming. We boarded the West Clock bus at the Utilidors entrance and headed over to the costuming building. Having trainers there who knew the costumes you were looking for was great. If I didn't have them there on that first costume run I would've been lost. They pointed us in the right directions, told us things like, "oh, that always runs small so get one size up", then also made sure we had all the right pieces to complete our outfit.

At that point the day was all but over. It was a long day but nothing too crazy. I basically had a walking tour of Magic Kingdom and then had a more in depth tour of Fantasyland. Plus I got paid while doing it! Not too shabby.

The next training day is another overview as well. This time it is land and role specific. So mine was an orientation to Fantasyland attractions. Which is a lot of attractions by the way. The most of any land. When you think about it you have lands within lands there. While Fantasyland is the overall land the smaller sections within it included Old Fantasyland (this was also known as the courtyard where you would find the classic rides like it's a small world and Peter Pan's Flight), New Fantasyland (which opened in 2012 with Under the Sea ~ Journey of The Little Mermaid and Enchanted Tales with Belle), Enchanted Forest (this was Mine Train, the Many Adventures of Winnie the Pooh and the Mad Tea Party) and then also Storybook Circus (The Barnstormer, Dumbo the Flying Elephant and the Walt Disney World Railroad station could be found here).

So yeah...a whole lot of attractions. The names of the areas aren't known by most of the guests but cast members use those names alot. It can be a little confusing because some of the interior lands just start with no indication but you get use to it. One way to tell if you are in a new area is to look at the costumes of the cast members. New Fantasyland and Enchanted Forest share the same outfits but Old Fantasyland and Storybook Circus have their own unique ones.

My group of about ten had two awesome attraction trainers walking us around the land that day. It started bright and early in an empty park. We walked through a couple of the queues where we got an introduction to how the FastPass+ touch points would work. Plus we got to see how FLIK cards worked. These have since been phased out for the most part but they were the red cards cast members would hand to guests and instruct them to hand them over to the cast member right before they board the attraction.

FLIK stands for Front of the Line Indicator Keeper (some say it actually stands for Fabulous Line Indicator Keeper). But basically the way these work is, there is a box at the beginning of the line. The box will beep and when it does so a cast member will grab a FLIK card, touch it to the box and ask the next guest in line to carry it with them as they wait in line. The guest then gives it to a cast member right before they get on the ride. That cast member touches the card to an identical box which can see when that card was last touched and determine the wait time associated with it. FLIK cards are deployed every few minutes and it's just one of the many ways that helps Disney determine wait times at attractions.

These things, seeing how the sausage is made so-to-speak, always piqued my interest. It was like my first days back at the Yacht & Beach Club. Up until this point I had only been privy to the hotel side of operations. There was still the world of the theme parks I knew nothing about.

The rest of Fantasyland Attraction orientation included stopping by some backstage areas so you could learn the best way to get from point A to point B. Then we were also shown some of the breakrooms we would be able to access. Breakrooms like the one for Peter Pan's Flight were so tight, old and dark, it seemed crazy to think cast members would actually enjoy a break back there. While others like the breakrooms at Be Our Guest, Storybook Circus and Journey of the Little Mermaid were all pretty much brand new and much larger than the closet of Pan.

I knew the Magic Kingdom like the back of my hand. It's a place, before my college program, that I had been to dozens of times. I could navigate any which way with ease. But adding in this new element of walking through backstage areas, through the Utilidors and knowing the best ways to get from here to there as a cast member brought a new thrill to the Magic Kingdom for me. The Magic Kingdom was now like "A Whole New World" for me to explore. I was excited to get started.

The day ended with the entire group getting to ride Seven Dwarfs Mine Train together. I watched the cast members work as I waited in line to get a little glimpse of my future. Immediately I noticed it was going to be much more fast paced compared to Front Desk at Yacht & Beach. I was entering a place very different than what I had been used to.

CHAPTER THIRTEEN

Where a Million Diamonds Shine

Disney World is really truly its own World. With 60,000 cast members and hundreds of different roles, no two roles are going to be exactly alike. Well, I would come to find out that Front Desk and Attractions were two polar opposites. Really none of the routines I had working the Front Desk would apply to my role in Attractions. I would begin to realize this as my training days started.

Much like my early days at the Front Desk, my training days at Seven Dwarfs Mine Train started bright and early. In attractions there are several different procedures you have to know how to do apart from the daily tasks, mainly opening and closing procedures. Because of this your training includes working a few opening shifts as well as working a few closing shifts. Training itself was five days in total. Two opening shifts, two closing shifts and a middle shift. Day six of training is your assessment. You needed to pass this in order to have your first day alone.

I met my trainer outside the Mouseketeria. I was going to be training alongside another college program extender. We headed to Fantasyland to begin the day. Seven Dwarfs Mine Train is a unique ride. Not just because it uses a one-of-its kind ride system (each individual car rocks back and forth) but because it is one of the only attractions that you can completely walk all the way around with each side fully themed. Because of this the ride is pretty much one-stop shopping for the cast members. While the guests only sees the queue, the track and other visible parts, there is a whole working area not seen by the guests within arm's reach.

The Mine Train has its own breakroom just steps away from the load and unload section of the ride. In comparison to other places this break room is small. It has a few tables pushed together in the center of the room with seating for about twelve or so. There's a fridge, microwave and lockers to store your items. Right outside the breakroom is a cast member only restroom too. Basically, almost everything you need for your shift is. This meant you never really had to leave the attraction itself when you clocked-in.

At Yacht & Beach I enjoyed walking to the Jib and Jaw for my breaks. It was a way to remove yourself from the work so that you could recharge for a bit. At first I was a little skeptical about being surrounded by the attraction for the entire time I was on my shift. As I would come to realize this was much better though. Instead of one hour long break, in attractions you would get two 15 minute breaks and one 30 minute long break. I enjoyed having more breaks even if they were shorter. The shorter breaks also meant that it would be harder to get to the Mouseketeria and back. So having the breakroom so close gave you the ability to get the most out of your break without having to walk somewhere to start it.

So, our trainer walked us to the breakroom and even at six in the morning there were quite a few people getting ready to start their day. In the morning about two hours or so before park opening is when things start to get going at the Mine. The ride itself needs to go through system checks to make sure everything is working properly. Cast members with the opening shift are first required to perform a track walk. Here two cast members would walk the perimeter of the ride to make sure all emergency exit gates were closed and make sure that everything else seemed to be in place. They would meet in the middle and then walk back into the breakroom. Then another cast member would walk the length of the track itself. As they walked the track they were looking for a number of things but overall they just wanted to make sure everything looked good for the trains to run.

Each night trains are set backstage where matinence cast members would perform routine check-ups. Because of this one of the first tasks of the day would be to get the trains back on the track. The next time you ride the Mine Train look for the cast member standing at the unload section behind the podium facing you as you arrive back. This position in the morning is the one that would bring the trains back onto the tracks. They run through a process in tandem with a cast member in the Tower position (this is the one that watches all the television screens to make sure the ride seems to be running correctly) to get the trains back on the track. Typically they would start the day with five trains.

While this is occurring other cast members are doing several other tasks to make sure the remaining positions all have what they need to start the day. Our first day of training was more observing everything than anything else. Throughout our training we would go to a "classroom" in the backstage area of Journey of the Little Mermaid. This classroom was really just a room with a few tables and chairs pushed up against the walls. We were required to read sections and chapters of manuals for the ride. It was excruciating reading these things. I understood that a lot of it had to do with safety protocol and knowing this is important to the operations of the rides but, it was just so dull.

I've mentioned the word positions a few times in the previous paragraphs. Attractions cast members for the most part perform their roles on a rotation basis. Meaning they rotate from position to position. The positions help break up the monotony of the tasks you have to perform. Rather than checking lap bars for all eight hours of your shift, you would typically do that for 20-30 minutes or so and then be rotated to another position to do something different. Having these short bursts of different tasks would help you keep from going crazy. The bigger the ride the more positions they have. Any roller coaster is going to have a lot of positions and require a lot of cast members at any one point in order to run it.

The first day of training consisted of observing cast members as they performed each of these positions. We were just getting a feel for it all.

As the training days progressed our trainer would have us take over a position and perform the tasks of each. For the most part each position was pretty straight forward. There were a couple that were hard to get use to but overall nothing too crazy. The notion of doing different tasks every 30 minutes or so was something I had to get used to. As a Front Desk cast member your role for the day was your role for the day. At attractions that's just not the case. But like most routines it's just something that takes time.

While training is still extensive it's nothing compared to what was required of me at Yacht & Beach Club. When assessment day came I was confident in my ability to perform each station. It was the written portion and the questions that my trainer was going to ask me that had me a little worried. With the different stations it was straight forward. At this station you do this and you do it until your bumped to another station. The written exam part was more about the ride systems and how they operate and are created.

It wasn't that I had no interest in this, in fact I had a huge interest in it. As an avid Disney fan I am fascinated by discovering how things work. I was worried about this because of how I learned it. Knowledge of the ride systems was presented in the form of manuals. If you think a car manual is boring, you have never had the pleasure of reading a manual for a mile long steel contraption. You can't make manuals interesting. If they were interesting they wouldn't be doing their job. So I assumed, rightfully so, that in my reading of these manuals I had probably gotten distracted and didn't retain everything I probably should have.

Luckily, it didn't prevent me from passing! I was able to complete that and perform the duties at each station sufficiently. I had officially "earned my ears" and was ready to head out on my own. But this first day might have presented me with a few more nerves than my first day at Yacht & Beach. Maybe it was because there was less training or maybe because the Magic Kingdom seemed kind of daunting with its sheer size and amount of guests. In actuality I was probably nervous because of what might happen if something went wrong. As a Front Desk cast member if something went wrong a guest might get upset and you might have to move them to a different room or give them a price adjustment. If something went wrong at Seven Dwarfs Mine Train it might mean someone being seriously hurt. With anything new it's just something that compounds your nerves.

But there was no time to get nervous because my first day was right around the corner.

CHAPTER FOURTEEN

A Day in the Life of a Miner

Like I said, with any routine it takes time to get adjusted to it. After a few short weeks I was more than adjusted to my new role, environment and co-workers at the mine where a million diamonds shine. In the first few weeks others on the college program were trained and became full time cast members with me. Early on it became apparent that I was still going to be having the later shifts as most who are on the college program do. Sometimes those late shifts could last until one or two in the morning depending upon when Magic Kingdom was open until. But us college programers didn't mind.

On the very late nights at the Magic Kingdom, College Programers wouldn't start clocking in for their shifts until around five, six and even sometimes seven o'clock at night. Soon the other full time and part time cast members would clock out and it'd be just a mine full of College kids. This was always fun. We grew to get to know each other really well and the late shifts were always a place that the college programers would own. Just like the more senior level cast members with years of experience would own their bright and early shifts.

A typical day would mean arriving at the West Clock Employee parking lot about 30-40 minutes before your shift was to begin. You'd hop on the West Clock bus and be taken into the Magic Kingdom. Now with the expansion of New Fantasyland in 2012 a new bus stop was constructed right behind the new addition. This stop was before you got to the entrance of the Utilidors but it was right behind Seven Dwarfs Mine Train. I'd get off there and then walk on stage to a back cast member only entrance into the Mine. As you enter the door you are greeted by the muffled singing of Doc, the defacto leader of the Seven Dwarfs.

"High Hoooooooooo!"

If you've ridden this ride before you know Doc starts singing this as you are in the Mine section of the ride itself. This is where the ride turns from roller coaster into almost a dark ride. Off to your left as you begin to ascend the second lift hill you encounter on the ride you'll see Doc counting some of the gems the other dwarfs have collected. Once your train gets to him he begins his bellow and soon the other dwarfs join in singing, "high ho, high ho, it's off to work we go."

This action took place above you as you enter backstage. The hallway you enter in is just a normal looking hallway. You don't see any of this taking place but because it's so loud you can hear it all occuring. Personally I always thought this to be a cruel joke by the Imagineers when they designed this ride. Imagine walking into work everyday and being greeted by a sing-song of "it's off to work we go". I am acutely aware that I am on my way to work, thanks very much!

If we're being honest it is actually a pretty cool way to start your day. You are here. The dwarfs are welcoming you. Now let's get to work.

After your greeting with the dwarfs you'd make your way to the break room. Off to your left you would catch a brief glimpse into the station where you would analyze the level of madness you were about to encounter that day. A few more steps gets you into the break room where you'd put away your bag, put your food in the fridge if it needed to. Right next to the door is a computer station. Here you would put in your "perner" number which is just your personal identification number that is associated with you once you get hired. Think of it like your Disney Social Security Number. You would type that into the computer and hit clock in starting fifteen minutes before your shift was due to begin.

Once it was your time to start you'd head back to the computer, put in your perner and then this time you would hit "get assignment". Your assignment would pop up on the screen which would prompt a receipt printer next to the computer to print off the tasks. One of three things would happen when you would hit get assignment. You would either pull someone's break or pull their "bump out" (bump out just means it's time for them to clock out). This means you would go find the individual and then switch places with them at whatever station they had. They go to their break or head home and you start with that position.

You could also pull rotation. Basically every station is a part of a rotation. Meaning one would go to this station which would then be followed by such and such station when it was time to rotate. If you pull rotation you would go to the first station listed and then send the person currently working their to the next station. The process would continue until the last station where that person would go in and pull a new assignment.

The third thing you could pull was a task. A task would be something like go sweep the queue, or go assist at this position and sometimes a task would be go make a magical moment. This would mean go find a family and walk them to the front of the ride without having to wait in line. Always a fun thing to do! Pulling a task was the computer's way of saying no one needs to go on break, no one needs to leave and rotation doesn't need to happen yet so go do this task until one of those things needs to occur. A task would last for about fifteen minutes, sometimes thirty, and once done you'd go back to pull another assignment.

Working at the Seven Dwarfs Mine Train meant you had a lot of positions you could be put at to work. Here's each position you'd have the potential to work at during your shift.

Greeter

This one is simple enough. You stand at the stand-by entrance to the ride and welcome guests as they enter. You would answer their questions about the ride, some guests might see you and ask you a question about anything at the park and sometimes you would just chit chat with a guest as well. You would also be required to check child's heights to make sure they were tall enough to ride. Every fifteen minutes or so you would also spiel to the guests waiting in line. The spiel would let them know what to expect. Keep up with the party in front of you, let the cast member know how many in your party and to keep in mind that the ride was two to a row.

You would also schedule come back times for those with the Disability Access Service. This would allow the individual to come back at a later time and go through the FastPass line. The way this worked is an individual (with a disability) would sign up for it at Guest Relations at the front of Magic Kingdom. They would then go to a ride they wanted to ride where the cast member would take their Magic Band or park ticket and scan it with an iPhone like device. It would then say the come back time which the cast member would recite back to the party and ask if that was ok. If it was the time would be booked. The time was based on whatever the current wait time was minus ten minutes. So if the wait time was 60 minutes, the comeback time would be in 50 minutes. The minus 10 was the thought that that was how long the FastPass+ line was probably going to take. Additionally they were only allowed to make one of this at any one time. They would have to use it before they could get another.

I loved working Greeter because for the most part it was pretty laid back.

FastPass+ Entrance

This position was right next to Greeter but would require you to stand behind a podium. Where Greeter might have been laid back this position could be incredibly stressful. You would make sure everyone touched their Magic Bands to the readers and then check the screen on your podium to ensure they had a FastPass+ for the current time. Every once and awhile someones "wouldn't work". That would mean you would have to turn them away. Sometimes you'd get people complaining that the line was too long so they wanted to go through the FastPass+ line. Sorry, no FastPass+ line for you.

You would have to take a hard line because letting people in without a FastPass+ just wasn't fair to those who actually had one and to those waiting in the stand-by line. That isn't to say every once and awhile I wouldn't just let someone on because of the mood I was in. Sure I'd do that but you can't constantly do that or the system would get backed up.

The challenge was always when someone's did not work and then they started giving you some long crazy story about how they should ride. You have to listen to their story while also letting others through the line. It could get very hectic and this is where occasionally guests were at their worst. For many they thought because the line was so long that they couldn't wait in the stand-by line. They would say they couldn't but what they really meant was that they didn't want to. If you don't have a FastPass+ then you always have the option of waiting in the stand-by line. The best thing to do in these situations was take a deep breath and be calm. At the end of the day if someone is getting incredibly upset that they have to wait in a line to ride a two minute and 30 second roller coaster, then they probably have bigger issues they need to handle internally.

This position was great 90% of the time when people with legitimate FastPass+ reservations would come through. Everyone was excited to ride Seven Dwarfs Mine Train and it was great to see people, especially kids, happy as they were going through the FastPass+ line.

FastPass+ Merge

For most attractions at Disney World once you scan your FastPass+ at the entrance you'll make your way down the line and then be required to scan it again. Where you scan it again is called the merge point because it's here where you will merge with the stand-by line. The role here is simple for the most part. Have people scan their Magic Band or ticket again and then let them proceed to the line. At this point you are also having those in the stand-by line hold. The big thing to consider here are your ratios. Meaning you needed to make sure the right amount of people were getting through from the FastPass+ line so that it was actually going quickly and working like it was supposed to. At times you would get a burst of FastPass+ individuals which required you to let more people from that line go through and hold the stand-by line for a little longer.

As many FastPass+ individuals were going through those in stand-by were just watching this happening.

So eventually they could get a little testy. But you just had to ensure to hold up the FastPass+ line every once and awhile in order to make the stand-by line continue to move.

The other factor you needed to do was ask each party how many people were in their group. Odd numbers would then be placed in a line and even numbers would be placed in another. I'll explain why this would occur in a moment. All you really had to remember with this was when anyone asked "why do we have to go in this line?", "because you're odd" isn't the best wording for a response. A couple times I had people look at me like they were offended I would always quickly realize my error and correct myself by saying, "I'm sorry, you're an odd number party!"

Depending upon how many people were working at the time of day there might also be a second position here called Merge Assist. Typically they would just split up the role with regular FastPass+ Merge. One would let people in and the other would hold the others in the stand-by line.

Wheelchair Assist

Anytime a guest in a wheelchair would come in from the FastPass+ or stand-by lines you would assist them. They would be put into a special section of the line. If they could stand you would have them wait and then take their wheelchair and park it at the exit of the ride so that they could collect it afterwards. If they couldn't stand then you would assist them with getting on the ride. The last car in each train had a door which would allow the guest to get in easier. Once that was done you could wait to help them get off or tell a fellow cast member at unload what train number they were in.

When Merge Assist was dropped from rotation due to low staffing numbers, Wheelchair Assist could also help the Merge cast member when there were no guests in wheelchairs that needed assistance.

Grouper

This position was the bane of most cast member's existence. The concept seems straightforward. As the guests approach you, you ask how many they have in their party. The trains hold twenty people in rows of two so ten rows in total. All you have to do is count up to twenty. Easier said than done.

At Seven Dwarfs Mine Train you had two lines that you had to deal with at this point. A line of even numbered parties and a line of odd numbered parties that were split up by the cast member at Merge. This was important because as you ask the even number parties how many in their group you could count by rows.

A typical exchange might be:

> Cast member: How many in your party?
>
> Guest: Four
>
> Cast Member: Rows one and two please. Two people in row one and two people in row two.
>
> Cast Member: How many in your party?
>
> Next Guest: Six
>
> Cast Member: Rows three, four and five please. Two people in row three, two people in row four and two people in row five.

When you get close to half the train filled with one line you'll want to switch to the odd numbered line. This one was a little tricker because you would have to group parties together.

A example of that would be:

> Cast member: How many in your party?
>
> Guest: Five
>
> Cast Member: Rows six, seven and eight please. Two

> people in row six, two people in row seven and one person in row eight.
>
> Cast Member: How many in your party?
>
> Next Guest: Five
>
> Cast Member: Rows eight, nine and ten. One in row eight, two in row nine and two in row ten.

Now once you got that down it was easy. You would just get into a rhythm and you couldn't be stopped. Where it got crazy was when the guests just wouldn't listen. They might go to a random row, decide they don't want anyone in their party to ride with someone else or even just start picking random rows. Like two people in a party would go to row one, two decided to go to row five and others in the party decided to go to the back row. One slip up like this could just initiate a waterfall reaction. Then everything else would get backed up. Trains wouldn't be filled, people would be separated from their parties and then people in line would have to wait while everything got sorted out. That's what always stressed cast members out.

Some were really good at Grouper while others just couldn't handle it. One cast member I worked with looked like they were going to have a mental breakdown every time they did it. Running back and forth screaming at guests to see how many people they had in their party. The one thing I learned which I've since carried with me, is that stress only breeds more stress. If you take a deep breath, maybe hold for one extra second and then start it's very hard to get flustered and it's very hard to have a full blown mess up. It was the position that everyone dreaded but it didn't have to be that way.

Station Assist

Luckily for Grouper they had a cast member who was there to help them load people onto the train. Once

Grouper assigned guests to seats Station Assist would make sure they were then escorted to the correct seat.

Communication between these two positions was always very important. Station Assist could let Grouper know how many more seats needed to be filled and also help organize the guests so that they were where they needed to be. Sometimes you get an extra group of two which Station Assist would put into row one. Then they'd let Grouper know that so that their counts weren't off. Being as helpful as possible for Grouper was the most important job for Station Assist. If you had two cast members working well together here, that meant trains were being loaded efficiently and guests were staying happy.

Front and Rear Gates

As you enter the train, sit down and look forward, the Gate cast members will be on your right. Front Gates was located before row one and rear gates was located after row ten (the final row). Once assigned to a row, guests would wait behind gates for their train to arrive. When the train came to a stop the gates would open and guests would enter onto the train. As soon as the last guest was passed the exit of the gates the Rear Gates cast member would push a button on the podium they were standing behind which would close the gates.

If a guest was taking longer than expected the Front Gates cast member would hold their hand out in the shape of a fist letting the Rear Gates cast member know to hold the gates open. As soon as the last guest passed through the gates, the Rear Gates Cast Member would push a button on the podium they were standing behind which would then close the gates.

If, for whatever reason, a guest wasn't able to get on before the gates closed there was a way to open an individual gate. Next time you are on Seven Dwarfs

Mine Train look right next to a gate and you'll see a little hole. Inside that hole is a button which when pushed will open the individual gate.

The other component of these two positions was making sure guests stowed their belongings and pulled down on their lap bar correctly. These are the "push up on your lap bar for me" cast members. Some guests understood what to do while others didn't. It was always a learning situation for some. If the guest pulled too far down on their lap bar and was uncomfortable the cast member could release the lap bar in little increments. This was done by kicking a section on the back of the car which would release the bar. The first few times attempting this were awkward because it was hard to tell where the spot was to kick. Eventually muscle memory would take over and I became a pro.

Front and Rear Load

Much like Front and Rear Gates without the gates. These cast members were on the other side of the track opposite the Gates cast members. Same position though, Front Load was above row one and Rear Load was after row ten. You'd check guests lap bars as well and make sure they were all comfortable. Typically you would split it up with the cast members at the front taking care of rows one through five and the cast members at the rear checking rows six through ten. Teamwork makes the dream work as they say!

One other point to make here is that each of these four positions had their own podium. Once all lap bars were checked cast members would go behind the podium and once the train was ready to dispatch a green button needed to be pushed. All four green buttons needed to be pushed and once they were pushed and held together the train would dispatch. Next to that button was a red button that you would basically hover your hand over. It was the emergency stop button. You would hover over it until the next train came into the load zone and stopped. This was just safety protocol. In case anyone ran near the track you were in a position to stop the train immediately by hitting that button.

Front and Rear Unload

Think of the load positions but in reverse. Only two cast members were required here. One in front and one in the back. This is less intense than the load positions. You would welcome guests back as their train came back into the station. Then once it came to a stop you would ask them to exit to their right and proceed through the exit gates. At these positions you also had a flashlight. Once each guest was off the ride you would go through each row and shine the flashlight to make sure the guests didn't forget anything.

Once that was all taken care of you would then go behind your podium and just like at load press the green button once it started to blink. This would dispatch the train from Unload to Load.

The Front Unload cast member was also in charge of putting trains back into the maintenance bay when the time came. Sometimes this was done while the park was still open with one or two trains going back there but once the ride was closed they would put all the other trains back there. It required a combination of button pushing and waiting for this to happen.

Tower

This is by far the most different position out of them all. In the back of the break room there was a door that lead into the Tower room. There a cast member would sit and monitor computer screens. These screens had live feeds of all the various cameras through the ride. A couple things would happen here. You would make sure all guests were remaining seated. If they weren't doing so you could get over the loudspeaker and remind them to do so. If it came to it you could also stop the ride until they sat back down.

A second component of your job here was being in touch with the cast members in the station. If a train took too long to load the Rear Gates cast member would call tower on their phone at their podium and say something like "train 5, long load time, wheelchair". That would basically mean that the last train that departs, train 5, took longer than normal to load and the reason was because a guest in a wheelchair was being loaded onto the train. You want to try and dispatch a new train every forty-three seconds. When you call in a delayed dispatch the cast member in the Tower would write that down and every once and awhile a coordinator would come in, get on the phone, and read off the times to another office at the Magic Kingdom. They would process that into the computer system which tracks efficiency for each attraction.

There are certain sections of the ride that might hold a train for an extended period. If it is taking a long time to load or unload a guest then another train might be held on a lift hill so that it doesn't dispatch into the train ahead of it. If it it held for an extended period of time the ride will require a manual dispatch. A beeping will start to go off which requires you to hit a button and dispatch the train from that section of the track. This would get everything back onto the right flow.

The third task you had was getting in touch with a coordinator if you had to. You might get a phone call from a fellow cast member asking if you could send a coordinator to the station to handle a problem. Tower had its own walkie talkie which you would use to track down a coordinator and send them out to where they were requested. This was probably the easiest part of the job but it was also cool because everyone in the Magic Kingdom used the same walkie talkie frequency. All of a sudden you'd hear "Splash Mountain is 101" meaning Splash Mountain was not operating. It was cool because it was almost like you were listening to something you weren't supposed to be hearing.

Tower was fun because you were able to get away from the hustle and bustle of the rest of the ride. It was quieter in there as well. The only stressful time was if the ride ever went down. If it did you were required to remain in there until everything was back running smoothly. Depending on what occurs you could be in there for awhile. But by then you'll have managers and coordinators in there to help you out.

Depending on the time of day and the staffing levels you could have additional roles in rotation as well. In the morning since the line is usually very long one role would be know as "End of Line". Pretty self-explanatory but you'd stand at the end of the line with a sign saying you were the end of the line. This helped with guest flow. Additionally other locations might get a second employee working there. Greeter 2 would assist the Greeter position and might walk around to see if guests not waiting in line needed assistance with anything else.

As you get more acclimated to your attraction you will inevitably have certain roles you will love more than others. I personally loved Greeter and towards the end I grew to enjoy Grouper as well. The Load and Unload positions were fun too but for the most part they were very close to being the same thing. Not a whole lot of difference but even one small addition to a task helps when you get rotated in order to break up the monotony.

You could anticipate being at one location for around 30 minutes or so until the next time you were rotated. Sometimes it was more and sometimes it was less. When the park was closing and everyone had gotten all their required breaks it was common to get stuck at one position for close to an hour or so. But the end of the night is usually less crazy than other times.

You never really knew how many or which positions you'd be doing in any given day. But that was part of the fun of working on attractions. You head in, do some positions, and then head home. In an already fast paced work location, rotation of positions only made your shift go by even faster.

CHAPTER FIFTEEN

Five Miles Away But Worlds Apart

One of the things I am fascinated with about Disney World is that it actually is its own unique world unto itself. The systems in place that are required to make the resort work everyday are massive and complex. From the transportation systems, to cooking of food or even washing of laundry, everything in Disney World is done on a grand scale. And it needs to be. Forty-three square miles (that's twice the size of the island of Manhattan), four world class theme parks, over 20 onsite resort hotels, 60 million plus annual visitors and some 70,000 cast members employed make Disney World its own unique place.

Despite all this it's easy for the average guest to not fully realize how different every role and location actually is. A guest can see a ride or a hotel and think it operates exactly the same way as the other rides and hotels in Disney World. Or they see a Front Desk cast member and an Attractions cast member and think their day-to-day must be very very similar. As you probably know by now that couldn't be further from the truth.

According to google maps it's about 4.7 miles from the Yacht & Beach Club to the Ticketing and Transportation Center at the front of the Magic

Kingdom. If driving it will take you about 10 minutes or so give or take. Along the way you drive on Disney roads and follow Disney signs to get you to your destination. You'll pass by other Disney resorts, you'll see Disney bus transporting guests and you'll see construction workers hired by Disney to build their next great thing. Everything you see will be Disney related and while your journey won't really take very long at all, for a cast member going from one destination to the next it feels like you're driving to a whole new world.

It's actually truly remarkable how vastly different the two roles I had were. Big picture of course they easily appear different on the outside. One works in a hotel and one works in the theme park. One checks people in while the other pushes buttons to make a ride move. But the small things, how the cast member's daily assignments went, those were probably the most different. Clocking in and clocking out and how breaks were handled are some of the smaller differences I experienced when making the jump from Front Desk to Attractions.

For me the biggest thing I experienced was a change in culture. Working at the Front Desk I think brought a much more professional level than working Attractions. Rightfully so, the Yacht & Beach Club is a AAA Four Diamond Resort and everyone working there needs to be upon the highest levels to continue that success. Attractions is a high paced, and depending of the guests, sometimes stressful job. Because of that it needed to be a little more laid back so the cast members can feel relaxed. But the management styles of my two locations were vastly different as well.

Working at the Front Desk you'd get to know your Coordinators (known as FSAs at the Front Desk) and your Managers very well. Some you'd like and get to know better than others just like any place you would worke. But for the most part it felt like you were all in this together. If you were working the Front Desk your coordinators would always be at your side to help in any situation. Your managers acted the same way. They would float from lobby to back-office to behind the desk but for the most part they would always be close to help. This was the same when you were working at curbside. Your managers for the day would come out and hang out with you for awhile and periodically check-in on you. Same thing with the Coordinators.

Yacht & Beach Club leaders just felt more welcoming in this regard. Even the Room Operations Managers (the manager of the managers) would make you feel welcome. Always saying hello and making sure you were doing alright. Some of my best memories working at the Front Desk included the times I spent interacting and learning from my managers and coordinators. When I was transitioning to Attractions I quickly learned that, that style of management wasn't always a given when working at Disney World.

At the Mine Train I would get to know several of the Coordinators very well and one in particular I would say I became good friends with. They really looked out for us for the most part. But a lot of the coordinators really didn't care to learn anything about you. They'd be friendly and what not but for the most part they'd just be punching the clock and going about their shift. For the most part this seemed to apply mostly to cast members on the college program. I'll give them the benefit of the doubt. It does suck getting close to someone only to see them leave a few months later. I once brought this up to my favorite Front Desk Manager saying something along the lines of, "wow I guess this happens every six months for you, a big group of people you've gotten to know just leaves." His response, "yeah, it really really sucks."

It's harder to miss someone if you never really got to know them. When you lean closer to full-time cast members you have that problem of saying goodbye less and less. Don't get me wrong a lot of full-time cast members are constantly transferring to different locations. But it's less of a guarantee than a college programer who has an expiration date attached to their employment.

Where it really differed was how you interacted with the managers. Leadership in the parks is broken down by role and then by location. As an example there would be a general manager of Fantasyland Attractions who has a team of managers working throughout Fantasyland. Then within each land it was broken down to sections. So a manager might be working in the Courtyard (Peter Pan, it's a small world, Mickey's PhilharMagic, Prince Charming's Regal Carousel) one day and then be working in the Enchanted Forest (Enchanted Tales With Belle, Seven Dwarfs Mine Train, Many Adventures of Winnie the Pooh, Mad Tea Party and Under the Sea - Journey of the Little Mermaid) the next day or would work at Storybook Circus (Dumbo the Flying Elephant and The Barnstormer). So for managers it was definitely a lot of ground to cover.

Coordinators on the other hand would only be working at one or two attractions a day for the most part. Because of how many people worked at Seven Dwarfs Mine Train it always had its own dedicated coordinators. That was a good thing, and was why you'd get to know your coordinators better than your managers. But sometimes I would go days on end without even encountering a manger and when I would it might just be a passing wave hello over anything else. Of course some were better than others but it just seemed like the managers didn't care about the people who they were managing as much as they should.

It's probably not fair to compare Front Desk Managers to Attractions Managers. Like I said Attractions Managers had a lot of ground to cover and Front Desk Managers were just at one hotel for the most part. Granted they did cycle through the Front Desk, curbside, Concierge and Club Level to make sure everything was going fine but at least they would engage with you when they did so.

Listen, I get that it's hard. There's an insane amount of cast members to keep tabs on and with college programmers cycling in and out it can definitely be tough to get to know all of them well. It's the difference from Front Desk to Attractions that I experienced that has always confused me. That at Disney World they can have roles with such different managerial styles from place to place. I wouldn't mention this if I didn't know that others felt that way too. Many of my roommates and other college program friends would lament about the same sort of stuff. "Yeah managers don't really care about college program cast members" was a common phrase. You'll always have great managers no matter where you go but changing that overarching belief is very hard to do.

On our last days at the Front Desk I had one manager take each cast member whose time was coming to an end for a walk. And on our walk together he asked what my future plans were and where I wanted to go. It was great to talk with someone who had grown their career already and hear their advice. At the end he made sure I had his contact information in case I ever needed anything from him. I thanked him for all of that and he said he was simply doing what so many managers had done for him. He was simply passing the torch.

My experience does not mean it's the same way for everyone. I am sure plenty of people have had incredible experiences with their managers working at Attractions and I am sure plenty have encountered the same things I experienced as well. It was going from Front Desk to Attractions where I really noticed the change.

I enjoyed my time at both for sure but I felt I grew professionally more working on the Front Desk. How I carried myself and how I interacted with my managers helped me in that regard. Working attractions helped me discover how to better manage stress and interact with people from all walks of life but my leaders weren't the ones responsible for that.

It was a little more cynical working Attractions than it was working Front Desk as well. I felt as if your fellow cast members were kind of egging you on in this regard. Like a mob mentality of sorts. Everyone took pleasure in bashing the guests backstage. It was a mechanism we all used to help reduce stress. But when it came to hating our job and vocalizing that hatred I tried my best to never take part in that. Complaining will get you nowhere and it certainly won't get you out of your present circumstances. I knew what I was getting into, for the most part, when I took a job in Attractions. I wasn't going to blame others for the situation I was in. All I was going to do was enjoy it as best I could. And I did enjoy Attractions, I'd be fine if I never had to work another day in Attractions in my life but now I look back on it fondly.

Having the opportunity to work two very different roles in a short period of time helped me learn a lot. I learned what it was like working with different management styles, how to handle stressful situations, how to think on my feet, how to be efficient and how to work with many different personalities. Work wise I wouldn't trade it in for any other experience. Thinking that a job at Disney World is going to be 100% magical and perfect is silly. Because at the end of the day it's still...just work. And even Disney can't make work 100% magical.

CHAPTER SIXTEEN

The Three Types of Disney Co-Workers

You might be surprised to find out that not everyone who works at Disney World is a die-hard Disney fan. Some, in fact, aren't really Disney fans at all. Working at Disney World is a job and people who fill those jobs come in all shapes and sizes. Even though Disney World employs more than 70,000 cast members, and there are more than 70,000 die-hard Disney fans in the world, that doesn't mean that everyone who works there will be one.

One can make a pretty compelling argument that Disney helped build Orlando and without their development of the Walt Disney World Resort it can be safe to say that Orlando might be a much smaller place than we know today. Disney contributes to incredible job production in central Florida. In both their on property parks and hotels as well as the off property hotels and businesses that benefit from the tourists Disney brings in. Because there is such demand for good employees, not everyone who applies for a job at Disney will be a fan of the company. Not that they are anti-Disney but rather that they just aren't huge fans like myself or probably you since you're reading this book.

That's what brings us to the three types of Disney cast members you will encounter at Walt Disney World.

The Die Hard

This is the cast member you want to believe is who populates every job position around the parks and resorts. For many in this group, myself included, they grew up loving Disney and knew that someday they wanted to possibly even work there. Their love of the company whether it be through films, shows, theme parks or a combination of any and all of them, drove their desire to achieve employment with the company.

For myself the parks were always the main catalyst for my love of Disney. When I arrived in Florida I knew that a big reason I was willing to work there was the desire to participate in the creation of the magic that I had experienced so many times before. That was my drive. Of course I wanted to work there to maybe kick-start my career with the company in another capacity but, I also really wanted to give back and make great memories for families visiting while I was there.

This isn't to say that these people are also of the mind that Disney can do no wrong. On the contrary really. These cast members can often be some of Disney's biggest critiquers. But the critiques occur out of love and a determination to make the company the best thing it can be. Sure you can complain about your job or the guests or co-workers from time to time but that's human nature. These are the cast members that are there because it's Disney and they want to be with Disney.

The Convert

Working for Disney is a great opportunity and few would argue against that belief. If you have the chance to work there you should probably strongly consider doing it as it can help you in many different capacities. To this day even though I only worked at a hotel and on a roller coaster people are still very impressed to see the Disney name on my resume.

This group of cast members understands that. They can be semi-Disney fans because it's hard to not like at least some aspect of the company. But overall their level of fandom isn't the reason they are working for Disney. You'll encounter this a lot with fellow cast members on the college program. For many they had never been to Disney World or never really knew anything about the parks. But they saw the program and thought it was too good to pass up.

They begin working and quickly become "true believers". "Traditions", the first class for every new Disney hire, typically helps push people into this category. They learn about the history and why and how the company has impacted so many people. It's hard for them to not completely fall in love with the place and the company. And this goes into their belief in the magic and how they carry themselves in the parks and their interactions with guests. They might have been wishy-washy to begin but not anymore.

The I'm Just Here For the Paycheck

Believe it or not, there are some cast members who merely show up and just treat it like a job. They don't utilize their benefits, like park tickets or dining discounts they just clock-in and then clock-out. They won't be fazed by the pixie dust and the magic. That isn't to say they aren't nice or they are mean to the guests. They just don't get caught up in the pageantry of working for Disney like most others do.

The fact is that you might see these cast members and think "what are they doing here?" But do you ask yourself that same question when you walk into Walmart or the grocery store or movie theater? Being a fan of a company isn't a prerequisite to work at a place.

Disney parks has almost made it that way though and for them that's a good thing. Through generations of incredible creations Disney has in turn created their own set of future cast members. Those that want to work there because of what it signifies. That's what makes so many of them want to go above and beyond what a normal job might entail.

There's no perfect science to these types of cast members. It just seems to be a common occurrence when you start working there. It's the willingness of the die-hards that often outweigh those who just treat it like a job. For the die-hards some days it is just a job and for the other groups some days the magic is real. But the diversity in the people you work with brings so many different types of overall people to you. Whomever they might be, their Disney fandom can vary.

The reason I bring this up is that I feel people often forget that, for how magical it is, Disney World is still a place where people go to work. Granted I would say it is a lot more fun to work at Disney World than many other places around the world but, it still is work. Going in with the mindset that every second of every work day is going to be carefree and truly magical is wrong. Going in with the mindset that you are eager and ready to work will get you much farther. The former mindset can become a tough reality to face once you realize "oh wait, this is actual work."

I loved my time at Disney World. I learned so much and grew professional and as an individual. What I also learned was that I wanted to go into the corporate world more so than wanting to stay and work in the parks themselves. My career needed to go elsewhere for me to find my passion and fulfillment.

If you're reading this book you are probably one of two people.

- A Disney Die Hard and/or
- My Mom

In the case I am not related to you, you have probably thought about working at Disney World at some point in your life. Or maybe you are even looking into the college program. If you do choose to work there, first off, great! I do still think and will always think working there is an incredible opportunity and a great time. But do keep this in mind, "it is a job." Work as hard as you can and then on your days off celebrate by spending time in the parks and interacting with other cast members. The days I had off and went into the parks helped me recharge my passion. I, as a guest, could see how other guests were enjoying their time. I would watch them interact with cast members and then come back with a smile on their face. Watching this would always get me going. I couldn't help but smile. It was a feeling I would carry with me into my days at work. To try and make it a great day and have a great interaction with every guest. The days which were tough could easily be remedied by going into the parks and seeing how what we as cast members were doing, meant so much to so many guests.

If you do work at Disney World keep these ideas in mind and understand that for some of your fellow cast members it might just be a job, but if you make it more than that and show your passion then you can make it a magical place for every guest you encounter.

CHAPTER SEVENTEEN

The Perks of Being a Cast Member

Working in the most magical place on earth of course comes with its own perks. And a lot of them! First and foremost has to be park admission. cast members can pretty much get into the parks as guests whenever they want. There are a few days throughout the year where cast members can't get into the parks, usually due to expected high crowds. But those days are few and far between.

For someone as Disney obsessed as myself, getting to go into the parks whenever I wanted was the best thing ever. Most places you work, one would never want to go there on their off day. Disney World is of course not like most places. Work could be a challenge at times. Long hours on your feet dealing with guest issues can really take a toll on you. Having the chance to cut loose and recharge your batteries was an incredible blessing. The parks gave you an incredible outlet to do just that.

For me, it was also a great way to constantly remind myself why I was doing what I was doing. The rough weeks could easily be flipped upside by a simple trip to one of the theme parks. Seeing a guest experience something for the first time, or watching them have a great interaction with a cast member was a sure-fire way to get your emotions in check. I loved doing this because it put me in a good mood and made me ready to face my next working day. Seeing is believing and when you see a guest having a great time you know that you as a cast member can be directly responsible for making sure that happens.

Before my college program began I had been to Walt Disney World some twenty times. Even with all those trips and living there and having the opportunity to go whenever, I never became bored with the parks. I always resented that notion too. When someone says "You're going to Disney World again? Aren't you sick of that place by now?", my answer is always "no". But I never understood why those same people who asked that question would go to the same beach year after year after year. How is it any different?

Moving down there was the same thing. "You're going to move down there? Won't you get bored with it?". Yet when someone says they are moving to New York City or Los Angeles or Chicago a response is never, "Aren't you going to get bored there?". I can't describe why I love Disney World. It is weird. But I do know that it is a place I will never get sick of.

Now thanks to living there I can't tell you how many times I've been to the parks. It is probably uncountable, and not just because I worked in one! Any chance I could get I would be in the parks. When you live there and have that opportunity you do begin to treat each trip differently. Before a trip would consist of a few days with the goal being to ride as many attractions and see as many things as you possibly could. It was strategic, tactical and days lasted very long. Up early and out late. My family would often joke that because there was so much walking you always needed a vacation after your Disney vacation.

Living there, your trips to the theme parks become quite different. Quick pop ins that only last an hour or two are often a common occurrence. Running from attraction to attraction is replaced with a leisurely pace as you stroll around the parks. Lines too long? No problem, there's always next time. Even though I had been so many times before there were still so many things I had never experienced because they just didn't make the list on my previous trips. The Liberty Square Riverboat became a favorite I would ride all the time when I was in Magic Kingdom. In Epcot I would explore every nook and cranny of each World Showcase pavilion, stumbling into places and discovering things I had never seen before. In Animal Kingdom I made my first trek out to Rafiki's Planet Watch aboard the Wildlife Express. In Hollywood Studios I'd stake a claim at a park bench on Sunset Boulevard while I sipped a beer and watched the "streetmosphere" characters interact with guests.

Everything isn't a must. In fact it was a common occurance to not really do anything when you went to the parks. Maybe you would hop on one ride or one show but sometimes I'd go to a park just to get a food item. On one occasion one of my roommates was craving a cookie. So we decided to go get a cookie....at Sleepy Hollow in the Magic Kingdom of course. Where else would you get a cookie? There is something to be said about going to a theme park just for a cookie. It was pretty awesome.

Getting to go to the parks whenever was awesome but getting to share Disney World with family and friends was even better. As a cast member you get a certain number of complimentary guest passes that allow you to bring family and friends into the parks. As with most things at Disney, college program participants were under their own set of rules when it came to guest pass allotment. On my first program I was given a certain amount and once I used them that was it. On my second program the number of guest passes you got was based upon the hours you worked. So you would get some in the beginning and then when you worked a certain amount you would be sent more. Disney is always tinkering with this it seems so if you are considering working there, it's best to just bring it up with your supervisors when you start.

I love going to the parks by myself. It was one of my favorite things to do. But sharing Disney World with your loved ones always is the best way to do it. It's a place that is meant to be shared with others. To laugh and enjoy each other's company in a place where families are really celebrated. My family had been to the parks many times before. So, of course, they appreciated getting in for free whenever they would come and visit me. Know there are certain blackout dates for your guest passes. Usually, they coincide with the busiest times of the year but that just gives you more reason to have your family come down when it is less crowded. The guest passes are probably the top perk for any Disney fan working in the House of Mouse.

What would I typically do with my paycheck from Disney you ask? Well, I would turn around and give it right back to them of course! Whether it was food or merchandising as a passionate Disney fan, of course, I was going to be spending a lot of my paycheck on Disney related things. Luckily, as a cast member, there were certain perks that could help soften the blow of these purchases. cast members get discounts on merchandising and on dining at certain locations. The percentage of the discount, especially food-related ones, would vary from place to place but some, in particular, were incredible.

Trail's End at Disney's Fort Wilderness Resort was a cast member favorite. They have an awesome breakfast and dinner buffet and some great options for lunch. At certain times these meals could be as much as 40% off for cast members! While 40% was an uncommon occurrence, it couldn't have been offered at a better place. Since my cast member days Trail's End has still remained one of my favorite places to eat in all of Walt Disney World.

Around the holidays cast members receive a special "bundle" of additional perks called the Disney Family Holiday Celebration. These included some coupons you could use for things like a free popcorn or soda in the parks. But the real kicker are the three dining coupons you would get. There was a 30%, 40% and 50% off coupon you could use at certain restaurants. These coupons in particular would have the most participating restaurants and were always a great deal. My family visited me once and I was able to use the 50% off coupon at Yachtsman Steakhouse in the Yacht Club Resort. At an expensive signature restaurant like Yachtsman, that's an incredible deal!

The Disney Family Holiday Celebration would also give you things like a free round of miniature golf and even an additional One Day Park Hopper for a family or friend to use. There was even a certain time frame where merchandise was 40% off for cast members! The full details of this change from year to year but when you get that package in the mail you know it's going to be full of good stuff!

Sometimes the perks of a cast member go beyond free things or discounts. The access you get to Disney World as a cast member is always the main appeal for any Disney fan. Sometimes that access means you get to attend a cast member preview for a new attraction, show, land or event. Other times it means you get to go on a backstage tour exclusive to cast members. I was fortunate enough to participate in a few of these when I was a cast member. This does depending on your work location I should point out. All the ones I attended were organized by my managers at Yacht & Beach Club. I don't recall ever seeing any offers when I was working in Fantasyland on Seven Dwarfs Mine Train however. The incredible tours included getting to ride Space Mountain with the lights on, getting a backstage tour of Fantasmic! the Hollywood Studios nighttime spectacular and my favorite of them all was a behind the scenes tour of the Haunted Mansion. This last tour would make any Disney parks fan swoon with envy. I was able to walk the track and even step into some of the scenes like the Ballroom. It was so awesome and I was so happy to have experienced that.

The perks are definitely one of the best parts of working at Walt Disney World.

CHAPTER EIGHTEEN

Celebrity Encounters

Each year some 20 million people pass through the turnstiles of Magic Kingdom alone. Walt Disney World is the top vacation destination on planet Earth. In America it has become a right of passage for many families to take at least one trip there. Because of its popularity, it attracts people of all backgrounds, including celebrities.

I'm sure you've seen the Disney press releases or blog posts before about this or that celebrity getting their picture taken in front of Cinderella Castle. It seemingly happens all the time. When you work in the parks you are bound to have a few encounters with celebrities as well.

The first one I remember was the band Wilson Phillips. They were playing at Epcot as part of the Eat to the Beat Concert Series during International Food and Wine Festival. Because of its proximity to the park, they were also staying at Yacht & Beach Club. Their manager checked them in but my co-worker who handled the check-in claimed to be such a big fan that the manger called the band over. They were all very nice but I never thought I would continue to have celebrity interactions over the course of my program.

Like Eat to the Beat, the celebrity narrators of the Candlelight Processional would often stay at Yacht & Beach Club. I happened to see actor Blair Underwood and I was even able to check-in Ana Gasteyer of *Saturday Night Live* and *Mean Girls* fame. She was incredibly nice and seemed very down to earth. When a celebrity checks in and is deemed VIP, they are typically checked in, inside their room. So myself and a manager escorted her and her party up to the room and then completed the check-in on an iPad. This was cool because they were all asking questions and clearly very excited for their Disney trip.

Now the big celebrity sightings came once I was working on the Seven Dwarfs Mine Train. During the time it was the most popular attraction in Disney World and especially in the Magic Kingdom. As with the resorts, in the parks celebrities are handled a little differently. They almost always have a Disney VIP Tour Guide escorting them around. This just makes for better logistics and if they are "mobbed" the Tour Guides can usher them backstage. But mostly it is so they can easily put them onto the rides.

The "status" and comfort level of a celebrity determines how they are handled within the parks. Sometimes they were just walked down the FastPass+ line and placed on the train like the other guests. Other times they could be walked down the exit and placed on the ride with other guests. Now for the big time celebrities, they was a good chance that they would be walked down the exit and then they would board at unload. The train would proceed to the load station but the gates wouldn't open for other guests. This meant that they would have an entire train to themselves. All of this was usually on a case by case basis and would typically come down to the comfort level of the celebrity themself.

Once I was standing in the station when a celebrity was getting off the ride. My co-worker was trying to get through a gate with a wheelchair but the celebrity was in the way. The cast member said, "excuse me". The celebrity didn't hear. The cast member got a little closer and said "excuse me" again, only this time the wheelchair accidently bumped into the celebrity. This generated a responses of "oh I'm sorry!" and the celebrity moved out of the way. As this response was occurring you could see the eyes of my co-worker getting very big. She walked towards me and said, "Did I just bump Shakira with a wheelchair?!" Yes, they did indeed bump into pop star Shakira with a wheelchair. Her husband, spanish soccer player Gerard Piqué, and her family were in Magic Kingdom for the day.

Sometimes it wasn't so easy to spot the celebrities. On one occasion as I was working rear gates I noticed someone with one other person and a VIP Tour Guide, waiting in the wheelchair section. His face looked very familiar. After a few glances back I was sure who it was. I picked up the phone and motioned for my fellow cast members at load to pick up the phone. Once they did I said, "I think Nick Cannon is waiting in the wheelchair line". A couple minutes and a few co-worker confirmations later, and Nick Cannon was all secure and ready to ride.

Depending on what position you are working at determines how "in the know" you might be when a celebrity comes in. As I was working Fastpass merge one day, a loud scream occured. Followed by a few more screams coming from other guests. I turned towards the station where Kylie Jenner and, at the time, boyfriend and rapper Tyga were getting on the ride. Of all the celebrities I saw during my time working in Disney, this was by far the biggest guest reaction I ever experienced.

The final celebrity story I have to tell also happens to be the most famous. In fact he's probably one of the most famous people in the world. I was walking in the load and unload area going from one place to another when I saw a full train dispatch from unload to load and then onto the track. The strangest part about it was that the entire train, all 20 seats, were filled with adult men. Not a woman or child to be see. Just then my coordinator comes up to me and says, "I can't believe Prince Harry is riding the ride right now." "WHAT?!?", I thought. Then I remembered seeing a red headed man in the last row. Prince Harry is involved with an organization called the Invictus Games. Each year the games welcome wounded veterans from all over the world to compete in Olympic style competitions. That year it was taking place in Disney World at the Wide World of Sports which is why the Prince was in town.

There was one aspect of that story that I will always remember. My co-worker, let's call him Chris, was working at the greeter position when Prince Harry was riding the ride. As his whole party exited the ride and walked out of the gates Prince Harry was all the way in the back. He walked back out into Fantasyland but then stopped, turned around and walked back to the greeter position. He went up to my co-worker and said, "Hey Chris, thanks for letting us ride I really appreciate it and it was a lot of fun. Have a good night!". That will always stick with me. He could've easily kept walking but he felt compelled to stop and thank the cast member. It was a total class act from the Royal.

So what have we learned today. The next time you're in Disney World, to paraphrase the Tomorrowland Transit Authority PeopleMover, "always keep your eyes open cause you never know who you might see."

CHAPTER NINETEEN

The Magical Moments

Yes you get your perks working as a Disney cast member and occasionally you might even run into a celebrity. But for me the best part of the job was how you can make an impact on a guest's trip.

I said before how I treated my time on the college program as a way to repay all the other cast members who came before me. This was a way to give back. I had been impacted by so many cast members on my trips there that I wanted to be able to have the same impact on guests as well. Being able to do this was what I loved about my job the most.

Sure there are the stories you see everyday. The little kid gets off the ride looks right at you and says, "that was awesome!". Even though you had nothing to do with building it you of course take credit for it and respond with, "Sweet! Glad you liked it!" Or when the guest comes to check-in and you are able to get them a better room, or fulfill their requests. They are ecstatic and you feel good because they are happy. These sorts of things can happen really anywhere at any sort of job. But at Disney the magical moments where you're allowed to go above and beyond are what really stick with you.

One day working on the Mine Train a family came through the FastPass+ line. It was a Mom, Dad and two girls. You could tell that the older girl was a little afraid. Which actually wasn't totally uncommon for the older sibling to be afraid and the younger one to not be. I think it has to do with the fact that the younger a child is the less they can actually comprehend what's going on. But what this came to was the older girl not wanting to ride. The Mom waited with her and you could tell she was disappointed. Mostly because she didn't want her daughter to miss out on anything. The girl just stood by the exit holding back tears until her Dad and sister came back from the ride. I decided to do something to turn the situation around.

At the FastPass+ merge point we had a small lock box that we would put paper FastPasses in. Paper FastPasses were still used for Rider Swithces and if a rode ever broke down cast members would hand them out as a make good so guests could come back and ride again. These were pretty much good for any ride at any time. So I walked over to the box, reached in and pulled out a paper FastPass. I went over to the little girl, bent down to get on her eye level and said, "It's ok to be afraid, but I don't want you to miss out on riding anything with your sister. So I want you to take this FastPass and go ride any ride you want with her, sound ok?". She started to smile and said, "ok" to me. But the Mom was very happy. She thanked me and said it was a very nice thing to do.

Now I don't tell this story to pat myself on the back, I tell it to prove a point. At Disney you are expected to go above and beyond to make the guest have the best possible experience. Technically I wasn't allowed to reach in and pull out a paper FastPass but I also knew that because of the situation if any manager or coordinator saw me doing that, they wouldn't say a thing. Because in that instance there are more important things than going 100% by the book.

One of my most proudest moments I had when it came to guest interactions was when I worked the

Front Desk at Yacht & Beach Club. I was checking in guests when a lady came right up to me and said, "Hi so we're checking and I'm here with my sister and all she wants to do is meet the Beast. Last year we weren't able to and that's all she wants to do, so how do we make it happen?".

"Wow", I thought. She came in hot! A lot of questions right up front. "Let's get you all checked in and make sure everything is all good and then I can give you some tips on where the best places to meet the Beast are." Throughout the check-in process I came to learn more and more about her. Turns out that she was there with only her adult aged sister who had special needs. Her sister couldn't speak but she loved Disney and clearly going to Disney World was a huge deal for her. I dug a little deeper and found out that her favorite character was the Beast, hence the infatuation with needing to meet him. The pieces were All-Starting to come together.

Now the Beast is a popular character and the film Beauty and the Beast is of course a Disney classic. Regardless of this popularity the Beast is actually a very difficult character to meet. Even with his castle being added to the Magic Kingdom in the New Fantasyland expansion and getting a signature dining experience themed after his ballroom in Be Our Guest, he is still a hard character to find.

I gave her the rundown of the best places to try to have her sister meet him. I explained how there was a show in Hollywood Studios, Beauty and the Beast-Live on Stage, where they could catch a glimpse of him. In Epcot sometimes he and Belle would do a meet and greet outside the France pavilion but that wasn't really consistently scheduled. They could see him make appearances in the Festival of Fantasy parade in Magic Kingdom. Then during dinnertime they could meet him at Be Our Guest restaurant. Now at the time, are really still to this day, Be Our Guest was the hardest dining reservation to get. So that was going to be pretty difficult to do. But I explained all the options to her and she was grateful for that.

A few days pass and I run into them as they are making their way back to their room. Of course I had to ask, "So have you been able to meet the Beast yet." She let out a sigh and said, "No...haven't been able to do that yet. We can't seem to find him anywhere where he is meeting people." I ran through the options once more and then I said, "Ok, what you can do is go up to the Be Our Guest hostess stand and beg them. Say all you want to do is meet the Beast, take a picture and then leave. If all else fails try that because just asking can never hurt." She agreed and said if it came to it she would give it a shot.

My shift went on and there was just something in my head that saying "Do something about this". There had to be a way for them to meet the Beast. So I went up to my coordinator explained the situation and then asked if there was anything I could do. We came up with a plan. The first step was to head over to our gift shop at the Yacht Club and see if there was any Beauty and the Beast merchandise. My coordinator gave me some money from a till and wrote it out as a guest gift so that I could go buy something. I ended up finding a pin, candy and a bookmark all themed to Beauty and the Beast. I bought them all then went up to their room. When they answered I handed them the gifts and said, "This is all from the Beast. He just wanted to say he's excited that you are here and that he will be meeting you sometime this week." They were very excited!

The next steps involved reaching out to entertainment at all the parks to see if there was a way to set up a meet and greet. I walked around with the number for entertainment written on a notecard for about a week. And I mean I had it on my person at all times. Every now and then I would call and see if there was anyway. No dice each time. I was starting to feel upset. Then one day I was working the Front Desk and I saw the lady I had been interacting with in the lobby. She had left her sister in the room and wanted to come tell me something. I was about to tell her that I had been trying to figure something out. Before I was able to explain she said, "Guess what? We meet the Beast!".

I was shocked! I came to find out that they did the last ditch effort I had told them to do. They went up to the Be Our Guest hostess and just begged to meet the Beast. They said ok and lead them inside. They got to meet the Beast and got their photo taken with him. Then as they were wrapping up a cast member at Be Our Guest said, "Would you by chance like to join us for dinner as well?" Can you believe that! They even got to eat there with no reservations. The cast members at Be Our Guest get all the credit. They saw what I did. They were just in the right position to make that happen.

Once she was done with the story she just wanted to give me a hug and say thank you for everything. I told her I was trying to get something done for them but she was just happy that someone cared enough to try and make it happen. She wouldn't have gone up to the hostess unless I had formulated that idea to her. She was over the moon and I knew I did the right thing.

Being able to try and get something like that done was awesome. Giving guests, who are nice and deserving, what they want was an incredible thing to be apart of. You realize that these trips are so much more than just vacations for many families. A trip to Disney World is a trip to a place where memories are made. Where loved ones can spend quality time with each and in some cases, like meeting the Beast, it really is a place where dreams come true.

That experience is one I will never forget and I can pretty confidently say that the two ladies I helped will never forget it either. It's the exact reason I wanted to become a cast member and was so excited to be a part of something like that.

CHAPTER TWENTY

The Not-So-Magical Moments

It's not always about making dreams come true when you're a cast member. Sometimes you get placed in some really awful situations. People like to argue. That's just a fact. They like to argue to try and prove their point, the argue to try and get their way and sometimes they argue just because that's the way they are wired. A Disney World trip can be exhausting, I get that. That exhaustion can easily turn into frustration and who's an easy target to exert that frustration on? The cast member you're dealing with.

I don't think there is ever the right scenario to pick a fight with someone. But the environment of go, go, go can bred arguments. Especially when you work in a place as fast-pasted as the Mine Train. It was almost like you didn't have time to explain the situation to an angry guest which would just make the whole ordeal even worse.

Working as a Front Desk cast member your typical complaint would be about how far away a guests room was or how they didn't have a king bed when they wanted one. While these complaints were common the reactions to each situation varied. Really guests could run the spectrum when it came to how they handled situations. One guest might politely ask if they could get a king bed while another would demand a king bed screaming while doing so and yet a third might break out in tears. That was always the craziest part for me. The unknown of how someone was going to react.

The same went for certain instances on the Mine Train. Being a ride that had a height requirement, in certain positions you had to check how tall children were. When they weren't tall enough you had to let their parent or guardian know that they couldn't ride. The most common reaction would be "Oh well, maybe next year!". But of course some were totally offended by this. "I would never ever put my child in harm's way. He can totally ride!" was the response of one gentleman yelling at me when I informed him his child was too short. The height restrictions are there for a safety reason, you going against that is totally putting your child in a potential unsafe situation.

The unknown is what can get to you. Not knowing how someone is going to react can really wear on your anxiety levels. It's unfair to judge someone with a split second interaction. You don't know how their day has been going. Or what events lead them to explode at you. You have to just take it in stride. Anytime one of my fellow cast members would get upset at how a guest treated them I would always respond with, "hey, if they are getting that upset over a 2 and ½ minute roller coaster, they probably have some bigger issues we don't know about." While that's true there are instances when people are really truly just the worst....

Case in point. One day I was working on Seven Dwarfs Mine Train. I was positioned at rear unload when all of a sudden the ride stopped. Typically that means a sensor was hit or something occurred to put the ride in emergency shut off for safety reasons. At this point individuals must be evacuated from the ride vehicles. It only takes a few cast members to do that so all other individuals working head out to the entrance of the ride to let guests know what's going on. As I approached the entrance I could see a coworker having a disagreement with a guest. I stepped in and asked the guest what was wrong.

"What's wrong?! My kids are in danger, stuck on the ride! That's what's wrong. I need to go down there and get them immediately!" he yelled.

I responded by saying for his safety he had to wait here and that cast members were helping his kids get off the ride now. Then it got a little crazier because he piped up by saying, "Oh yeah? Well for your safety you better let me down there right now." I was totally taken aback but simply said, "Sir, is that a threat?". At this point the guy backed off but was still very upset. He was murmuring and flashing daggers my way until his kids got off the ride. "Oh good! You're alright!", he said to his kids (and their mother by the way who was with them the whole time!), "I've been busy dealing with Tweedle Dee and Tweedle Dumb over here," gesturing to my coworker and I.

In the moment I will admit it was pretty intense and even a little scary. Guests can do some pretty crazy things. But just a little while later in the breakroom me and my fellow coworkers were having a good chuckle over it. That's really all you can do.

Disney World is a place built on magical moments and if you just see the advertisements you think the place is non-stop happy. When it comes down to it, just like everywhere else in the world, that's just not the case. The sooner you are able to realize that the better. When you don't let the bad moments get to you, you are able to make the good moments, the magical moments feel even better. It takes two to tango and for the each magical moment there has to be a magical cast member and an equally magical guest.

CHAPTER TWENTY-ONE

A Place to Broaden Your Horizons

I don't think there has been a time where I have grow so much as a person before, than during my time working at Disney World. I came into my college program as an anxious recent college grad. When I left I was a much calmer person, I was so much better at knowing what was worth getting worked up over and what wasn't. Working in high stress environments can do that to you.

But the college program isn't just all about work. It's about living and being on your own too. I learned how to fend for myself. I become much more independent and comfortable taking care of my well being. When you move to a place hundreds of miles from home, where you know nothing about the area and you know no one there, you grow up and adapt pretty quickly.

Your coworkers, roommates and friends come from all walks of life and from all over the world. I have never been surrounded by such a diverse group of humans before. Getting to talk to your roommate from Chicago one second and then having a conversation with your coworker from Brazil the next was so unbelievably cool. You learn so much from each person. About their backgrounds, about their cultures and countries and even just learning so much about themselves. You begin to understand that all of us really aren't that different after all.

If you've ever wanted to perfect your communication skills then getting a job at Disney World is the place to do just that. Effective communication can help each guest fully understand what is going on and can help make your job much easier. Working in the parks you come across a whole lot of different languages. You have to learn to communicate with things other than your words. Knowing what cues and signs people understand can help you communicate better in your own language even. Understanding that not everyone thinks the same way also shows you the importance of treating each person like a singular individual.

No matter what task I was doing or what guest I was interacting with I came at it with the approach that, this was the first interaction they've ever had with a cast member. Almost always that wasn't the case. But what if you knew it to be true? You'd probably act differently, right? This is something I still take with me in my current job. Approach everyone with the same kindness and good attitude because you don't know what happened to them before they interacted with you. If they want to be mean so be it. But you should never be the one to initiate it.

It's crazy to think I learned all this working on a roller coaster. But it's true! I could easily come at it like I did a job where I pressed check-in on a computer or I pushed a button to send a roller coaster train. But it was so much more. It was about working in the busiest ride in the busiest theme park in the world. It was about interacting with guests and coworkers from all over and learning from them. It was about making memories last for every single guest you could. And it was about doing all this in my favorite place in the entire world. Disney World changed me. I wouldn't be who I am today without it. For that I am eternally grateful for it broadening my horizons.

CHAPTER TWENTY-TWO

Exploring Orlando

Broadening your horizons can go beyond the gates of Walt Disney World. After all, you have a whole area to explore in Central Florida. For as big of a Disney World fan as I was, one of the things I was most looking forward to when I accepted the job at Disney was getting to explore the area outside of property. I had been coming to the place ever since I was a young child and yet the only thing I ever really experienced was Disney World. Sure my family has stayed off-property a couple of times but even then it was just hanging at the resort then driving to the theme parks. Nothing else.

At that point I hadn't really lived in a whole lot of other places outside of Maryland where I grew up. So I was excited to see what Orlando had to offer. Overall, I feel like Florida gets a super bad rap. Probably because people are just jealous of the place. I mean the weather is beautiful year round, the cost of living is great and specifically in Orlando there is so much to see and do outside of the parks.

Of course there are other parks outside of Disney World to explore too. I remember one of my first days spent in Florida was going to purchase an annual pass for Universal Studios Orlando. I had never been and it was kind of cool to get an annual pass to a place I had never been before but, I knew I was going to love it. And I did! Is it better than Disney World? Of course not but, it does have some cool aspects to it. The theming is great and a lot of the rides are pretty incredible. But the Wizarding World of Harry Potter takes the cake.

I can't recall a man made place that has left me so in awe like Diagon Alley in Universal Studios Florida. The details and the theming immerse you fully in the world of not just Harry Potter but of the streets of London. Obviously the place doesn't actually exist in London but after visiting Diagon Alley it feels like it really should.

Other rides like Men in Black, Rip Ride Rockit, the Incredible Hulk and the Amazing Adventures of Spider-Man are incredible attractions in their own right. And I'd be remiss if I didn't mention the Revenge of the Mummy. That attraction isn't just one of my favorite at Universal Orlando it's one of my favorite attractions in the whole world. Love that ride. Spending so much time in the Disney bubble, with living, working and exploring the property, it was nice to "escape" to a different theme park every now and then. Universal Orlando definitely helped in that capacity.

The city of Orlando itself has some pretty cool places as well. Winter Park is a neighborhood just outside the downtown area that is very cool to explore. Probably one of the most affluent areas in Orlando, Winter Park has a great downtown area filled with shopping and dining. I would spend many a night there eating at one of the local restaurants, visiting a watering hole or just strolling around.

Then downtown Orlando has its own spots. Definitely more of a late night area with its contingency of bars, downtown could get pretty hopping on a weekend night. I had fun there a few times with co-workers as we looked to blow off some steam.

Just off Disney World property, Celebration was a town originally created by Disney as a centrally planned community. Disney has since given up jurisdiction of it but, the town still has its Disney touches throughout. More restaurants and shops are here for exploring.

All in all, Orlando is just a cool place in my opinion. It is definitely a spread out kind of city so you will almost always be driving 20 minutes to get somewhere. But having a car gives you the opportunity to go to so many different places with a short drive.

I think it helps being in an environment surrounded by people not from Orlando. If you move to a new city you are much more likely to go out and explore all that it offers than if you have lived their your whole life. Working at Disney you interact with a lot of co-workers not from the area. Because of that you could always find someone to go out and explore with you. That was one of the best things I got to experience. Exploring a new city and learning to love Orlando was not something I was expecting to happen but, I am glad that it did.

CHAPTER TWENTY-THREE

The Last Day

My grand plan of working for the company for my whole life didn't really work out. At some point I realized I probably had to head back home and figure stuff out. It was a tough decision but it had to be done. I planned to head back after my second program came to a close. Unsure of what I was going to do but knowing I had to leave Disney for the time being.

The last few days were tough. I tried to pack it all in. Saying goodbye to friends, staying in the parks as much as possible and visiting favorite Orlando spots one final time.

It's a weird situation because you'll probably never be in another instance where so many people around you are leaving a place of work at the same exact time. It's very much like semesters in college in that regard. I would always feel bad for my managers and full time coworkers who had to endure that every six months or so. A new group of college program kids would come in, you'd get to know them maybe even become really good friends with them just to see them leave in a few months. For many you'd probably never get to see them again either.

You grow very close to your fellow college program coworkers. At least I did with a lot of them. It's a place and a job that fosters close relationships. The high stress job gives you a lot to bond over together. For some you would often have the same days off. When the only people you really know in Orlando are your coworkers then they also became the people you hung out with during your days off.

Spending so much time with the same people can obviously make it super hard to say goodbye. It's one thing to have to leave Disney World but it's quite another to have to say goodbye to people you grew so close with at the same time. It's almost like you went to battle together. It is a bond that's just too difficult to explain.

I will always vividly remember watching the Magic Kingdom's fireworks, Wishes, with my fellow coworkers during one of our final days in the parks. There were plenty of 20 something year olds crying in the hub of the park after the show. I remember just chuckling to myself because I could only assume the regular park guests around us were probably very confused as to what was going on.

It could have been a lot worse. I know as the avid parks fan that I was, I would be back shortly as a tourist. While I didn't know if I'd ever get to move back again, I knew it wouldn't be long until I was back. But saying goodbye to the people was the hardest part for sure.

CHAPTER TWENTY-FOUR

What I am Doing Now

It was difficult to leave Disney. Both the company and the city of Orlando. My whole life I put myself on a certain path. One that would end with me spending my life working for the company, living in Florida and spending my free time in the parks. As I've grown I know that it was an unrealistic idea. Not because it was unachievable but because there is so much uncertainty surrounding it. You're at the mercy of a place that gets a lot of applications from a lot of people.

I could have stayed and worked in attractions or something like that, but I also knew that while I loved Disney I loved creating just as much. I work in marketing now and what I love about it is having the ability to be in a business unit while also being able to be creative. I write copy and create images to drive interest in the things my company sells. It's great and I really enjoy it. That's the kind of work I've always wanted to be able to do.

Yet Disney still calls me and one situation made me do something about it.

A couple months before my college program was up I saw a Facebook post from one of my favorite Disney World podcasts. It was a show I had been listening to for years. They posted a job description for a new member of their team. They wanted someone who was good with creating and editing videos as well as producing other content. Now, my video skills were limited but my creativing and my interest in video content was definitely something I had begun to explore in recent years. So with my college program winding down and unsure what I was going to do after I decided to apply. Much to my surprise I got an email back asking to set up and in person interview.

I was elated but also nervous. I didn't know if I had the skills necessary to do the job. But the interview was scheduled and I was excited for that. To say the first interview went great would be an understatement. Everything just came so naturally. It was like I was just having a conversation with the two people interviewing me. Talking about whatever we wanted to. Yes we talked Disney and we talked about content creation and my marketing background but it was all so organic. No forced awkward questions and no canned responses. In fact at the end the main interviewer said, "You know people are going to ask you how this interview went and you can let them know that it went very very well."

A second interview came a couple of weeks later. It was via Skype and this time more people were interviewing me. This one didn't go as well but I just kind of chalked that up to Skype and the lack of personality that can come across with it. That's just the nature of the beast when it comes to that. They said they would let me know in a few weeks if I got the job or not.

My heart sank the day the email popped into my inbox. It started out great. They really liked me. Of the original 150 applications they got they narrowed it down to 15 for the first interviews and then down to 2 for the second interviews. While they like my personality and my passion they had decided to go with the other individual because they had more actual film experience. I was heartbroken. Not just because

I wanted the job but more so because I knew that this signaled my time in Orlando was officially over. I could live with not getting the job especially since they went with someone who had more technical experience. It was something I just didn't have.

The last month of my college program came and went. I moved back to Maryland and got a job in Marketing. I immediately liked it but also knew if the podcast ever called me back or reached out I would drop everything to move back down there to work with them.

Over the next six months or so I starting missing Disney. I was clinging to a dream that I would magically get offered a job back down there. Until one day I came to a realization. Why was I waiting for someone else to dictate my success? I knew I wanted to have Disney be a part of my life and apart of what I did professionally. I thought back to that first interview and tried to think why it went so well. Then I realized it went well because I was just talking about my passions. My passion for Disney World and my passion for content creation and marketing it. I had a love of Disney and a love of creativity. If I could do that then I would be the happiest person in the world. But just like I was relying on Disney to give me a job I was also relying on the podcast to reach out and give me one to. (Let me just say I have no hard feeling towards anyone on this matter either. Both Disney and the podcast probably made the best decision for their own needs. Which is fine with me.) I discovered that if this was what I wanted I would have to go out there and make it for myself.

And that is exactly what I did. I built a website and started writing blog posts for it. Posts on anything and everything Disney World. I would share tips and tricks while giving reviews and telling stories from the parks. I'd take the library of pictures I had taken over the years and share them. Eventually I would partner with one of my best friends and start a podcast where we would talk about the Disney news of the week and share our opinions on it.

Growing up I would crave as much Disney World content as humanly possibly. I loved going on message boards and reading different trip reports. Living vicariously through other people's trips was a great way to appease my Disney appetite. What I probably enjoyed most about it all was the Disney fan community coming together to share their opinions on everything at Disney World. Everyone has an opinion on Disney World and each one helps shape our own unique Disney World experience.

That gave me the inspiration for the name I would choose. WDW Opinion is the blog and podcast I started that shares Disney World opinions with the world. We share our opinions and then the rest of the community shares their own. It's being going for a couple of years now and while it's not my occupation one day I hope it will be.

What's great about working on this is that I've taken the knowledge I learned working at Disney World and applied it to growing my platform. Storytelling, excellent communication, great customer service (I leave no comment unanswered!) and the politeness that creates a welcoming environment. It's cool knowing that it has come full circle in a way. Working at Disney World really lead my to where I am today. I am a strong believer in fate and that everything happens for a reason. The struggles and ups and downs have lead me to this point.

I may have left Disney World a few years ago but, that wasn't the end of my Disney journey. It was just the start. And I for one can't wait to see where it takes me. From Yacht Club to Diamond Mine and now to the internet. It's been a great ride so far!

About the Author

Conor Brown is a lifelong Disney fan who's been traveling to Walt Disney World for the past 20 years. When not in Orlando you can find him devouring all forms of content to learn the history, stories and tips about anything and everything at Walt Disney World.

As a former Walt Disney World cast member, Conor knows what it takes to make the Disney magic and he still applies what he learned while working for the mouse to his daily life.

Conor takes his knowledge as a cast member and his knowledge from two decades of visiting the parks and shares his thoughts and opinions on his blog and podcast. As the founder of WDW Opinion he has made it his mission to help his fellow "Opinioneers" plan for and daydream about their next perfect Disney vacation.

Learn more about Conor and his work by visiting WDWOpinion.com.

About Theme Park Press

Theme Park Press publishes books primarily about the Disney company, its history, culture, films, animation, and theme parks, as well as theme parks in general.

Our authors include noted historians, animators, Imagineers, and experts in the theme park industry.

We also publish many books by first-time authors, with topics ranging from fiction to theme park guides.

And we're always looking for new talent. If you'd like to write for us, or if you're interested in the many other titles in our catalog, please visit:

www.ThemeParkPress.com

• •

Theme Park Press Newsletter

Subscribe to our free email newsletter and enjoy:

◆ Free book downloads and giveaways

◆ Access to excerpts from our many books

◆ Announcements of forthcoming releases

◆ Exclusive additional content and chapters

◆ And more good stuff available nowhere else

To subscribe, visit www.ThemeParkPress.com, or send email to newsletter@themeparkpress.com.

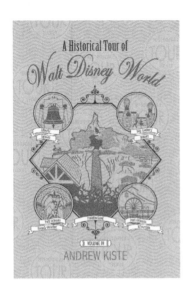

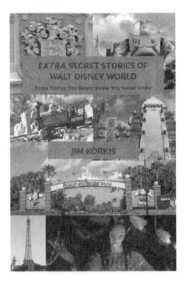

Read more about these books
and our many other titles at:

www.ThemeParkPress.com

Printed in Great Britain
by Amazon

42173668R00081